The Art of Healing

THE WISHARD ART COLLECTION

The Art of Healing

THE WISHARD ART COLLECTION

Cinnamon Catlin-Legutko

With Essays by Katherine C. Nagler and Hester Anne Hale

PUBLISHED BY THE INDIANA HISTORICAL SOCIETY PRESS IN COOPERATION WITH THE WISHARD MEMORIAL FOUNDATION, INC.

INDIANAPOLIS 2004

Printed in Canada

The paper in this publication meets the minimum requirements
of American National Standard for Information Sciences—
Permanence of Paper for Printed Library Materials, ∞
ANSI Z39.48-1984.

Library of Congress Cataloging-in-Publication Data

Catlin-Legutko, Cinnamon.
    The art of healing: the Wishard art collection / by Cinnamon
Catlin-Legutko ; with essays by Katherine C. Nagler and Hester
Anne Hale.
        p. cm.
    ISBN 0-87195-171-1 (alk. paper)
    1. Mural painting and decoration, American—20th centu-
ry—Indiana—Indianapolis. 2. Hospitals—Decoration—
Indiana—Indianapolis. 3. Mural painting and decoration—
Indiana—Indianapolis. 4. Wishard Memorial Hospital
(Indianapolis, Ind.)—Art collections. I. Title.

ND2635.I6C38 2004
751.7'3'0977252—dc22   2003061982

CREDITS FOR ARTIST PHOTOS:
PAGE 30, COURTESY JOAN WALLACE; PAGE 44 (TOP), COURTESY TODD ANDERSON;
PAGES 15, 18, 22, 39, INDIANA STATE LIBRARY; PAGE 8, INDIANA STATE MUSEUM AND
HISTORIC SITES; PAGES 25, 46, 47, 48 (BOTH), 49 (BOTH), INDIANAPOLIS MUSEUM
OF ART; PAGES 35, 44 (BOTTOM), LILLY LIBRARY, INDIANA UNIVERSITY, BLOOMINGTON

CONTENTS

DEDICATION

This book is dedicated to my husband Larry, who has watched this project grow over the past few years and has supported me during the journey.

THIS BOOK MADE POSSIBLE BY THE ST. MARGARET'S HOSPITAL GUILD AND WISHARD MEMORIAL FOUNDATION, INC.

Named for the story of a French princess who cared for children in her community, the St. Margaret's Hospital Guild was founded in 1907 to provide funding for the care of sick children in the community. Before the turn of the century, Indianapolis children were treated at Eleanor Hospital until it was destroyed by fire in 1909. After that, children were cared for and treated in the basement of City Hospital, now Wishard Memorial Hospital. The arrival of the Burdsal units in 1914 allowed for better care of pediatric patients as well as men and women. The ladies of St. Margaret's Hospital Guild took it upon themselves to beautify the new wards and inspired an unprecedented moment in Hoosier art history.

Today, the Guild continues its fund-raising mission for Wishard Health Services with the annual Decorators' Show House. Since 1962, monies raised through the Show House have funded the new Richard M. Fairbanks Burn Center, radiology, pediatrics, breast diagnostics, newborn and intensive care nurseries, ambulance services, and a mobile mammography van. In all, through the Decorators' Show House, St. Margaret's Hospital Guild has raised more than $8 million dollars for Wishard Health Services.

Wishard Memorial Foundation, Inc., is a public philanthropic organization dedicated to raising funds and awareness that support health-care initiatives benefiting residents of Marion County with special emphasis on its vulnerable populations. Since 1999, the Foundation has raised in excess of $8 million, including $5.7 million for the new Richard M. Fairbanks Burn Center and approximately $2.5 million more for such programs as Wishard's Senior Care's GRACE program for homebound seniors, Palliative Care for patients with incurable conditions, House Calls, the Hispanic Health Project, the George H. Rawls, M.D. Scholarship Fund for underrepresented medical students, Wishard's Level 1 Trauma Center, Prostate Cancer Screening, and for its own endowment.

The importance of the health care and services that Wishard Health Services provides to Indianapolis is undisputed. Through private gifts from individuals, corporations, and foundations, Wishard Memorial Foundation is helping meet the needs of our community's most vulnerable populations, making Indianapolis a better place for all of its residents.

ACKNOWLEDGMENTS

This project began in 1999 during the 140th anniversary celebration of the founding of Wishard Hospital. For the celebration, I was asked to curate a small, short-lived exhibition of the existing collection. This was the first time the collection had ever been exhibited together and it only hung for two days and was viewed by Wishard employees. Since then, the desire for a much larger exhibition with maximum exposure has been burning in me. Thankfully, the Indiana Historical Society felt this to be a wonderful story of Hoosier art and agreed to host the exhibition.

There are a number of people to thank. My greatest thanks go to Anne Emison Wishard who saw the potential of this project and has put her heart and soul into the conservation and future of the collection. As a member of the Wishard Memorial Foundation board, she has garnered financial support for this project locally and around the state. She has brought many of her friends to the project who share in her dedication: Tim and Kathy Nagler, Wayne Zink, Randy Deer, members of the committee, and her husband, Gordon Wishard. Thank you.

Dane Starbuck and the Wishard Memorial Foundation staff are to be commended for their support of this project. As Wishard Hospital's fund-raising arm, they have provided for countless projects that benefit patient care. With this project, they have identified another important component of the hospital, its history. Through their administrative support of the Art of Healing project, they have demonstrated the link between past and present and have opened new pathways into the philanthropic community. Thank you.

The Wishard Public Relations and Marketing staff has been an incredible force for this project. I thank you for your tremendous professionalism and sense of style. This project truly shines with your light. Thanks specifically go to Mary Minix, Michelle O'Keefe, Dana Scott, and Kim Harper. Your patience and talent has been an incredible asset. Thank you.

And to the folks at Wishard whom I regularly call upon to move paintings around: Gary McGowan, Bill Dugger, and Brian Rednour. And to those folks who have photographed these works at the wildest angles and locations: Mark Fredericks and Nathan Hurst. Thank you.

Over the next few years, the Indianapolis Museum of Art will restore these paintings to their original beauty. A couple of key staff members have been concerned about this collection and have graciously answered questions and assessed the condition of the collection. Thanks go to Martin Radecki and Linda Witkowski. In addition, the staff of the IMA library was very helpful during the research phase of this book. Thank you.

The Indiana Historical Society has shown great support for this project. Special thanks go to Sal Cilella, Tom Mason, Paula Corpuz, Cathy Bennett, Steve Cox, Ray Boomhower, George Hanlin, and Kathy Breen. Your advice and support have been influential. Thank you.

A special thanks goes to Patricia Prather, who has beautifully designed this book and created a work of art.

Before this project is through, there will be a multitude more to thank. I thank all of you who support the arts in you personal and professional giving. This remarkable collection of Hoosier art has a future because of your generosity. Thank you.

THE ART OF HEALING: THE WISHARD ART COLLECTION

Cinnamon Catlin-Legutko

*H*idden within the confines of one of the nation's oldest county hospitals is a historic and unprecedented collection of mural paintings. The art collection at Indianapolis's Wishard Memorial Hospital was originally created as murals that adorned the walls of patient care wards. Today, it hangs in public spaces, offices, and conference rooms throughout the hospital.[1] A total of sixteen prominent Indiana artists contributed to this mammoth 1914 project, resulting in an estimated quarter mile of artwork. Project supervisor and famous Hoosier artist William Forsyth regarded it as "the most ambitious and monumental work yet undertaken by Indianapolis artists."[2]

In the years since its creation, the collection has faded from public awareness. Age and misguided care have drastically altered the beauty of the murals, and what remains today is a fraction of the original project. The story of this great public work is a reflection of Hoosier talent and camaraderie joining to create "a great milestone in Indiana art."[3]

THE BEQUEST

y the early 1900s hospitals were gradually integrated into American cities. Health care in the early decades of the twentieth century was a dreary proposition. Illnesses and injuries usually guaranteed the patient a trip to the hospital for a prolonged stay. Patients were referred to as inmates and convalesced in wards shared by several patients with men, women, and children segregated into their own wards. Hospitals smelled of ether, iodoform, and human sickness with adequate ventilation at a premium.[4] Ward nurses were often young wide-eyed students receiving on-the-job training to complement their curriculum. Physicians, although scientifically trained, were rarely schooled in the art of bedside manner. Specialized medicine was emerging, however, as a transition from the family doctor who cared for all members of the family, whatever the ailment. Health care was developing as a scientific pursuit contributing to the decline, albeit slow, in mortality rates.

At the turn of the twentieth century, Indianapolis could boast of City Hospital, a civic building project that had struggled to exist since its founding in 1859. In the beginning, the hospital grew in fits and starts fueled only by occasional fears of smallpox and cholera epidemics.[5] By 1914, however, City Hospital began to look like a modern hospital with the completion of the Burdsal units, which came about as a result of a generous bequest to the city from a prominent Indianapolis businessman, Alfred Burdsal of the Burdsal Paint Company. A portion of the bequest was dedicated to the construction of "modern" patient wards at City Hospital. Burdsal intended the wards to be used by patients unable to pay for health care.[6] The project began in 1911 while Mayor Lew Shank was in office. During that same year Dr. T. Victor Keene became president of the City Board of Health and was immediately dissatisfied with the building plans, feeling that the rooms were both too small and poorly planned. Keene and Shank wanted the architect dismissed and the project started anew.[7]

The American Architectural Association was consulted and a contest was staged to solicit proposals for the new ward buildings. The Indianapolis firm of Anton Scherrer was awarded the project for its use of a modern design.[8] Scherrer acted as the mechanical engineer, while the architect was Jacob Edwin Kopf. The Burdsal units were of prairie style design and were originally two buildings that stood independently on the west end of the growing hospital cam-

Burdsal units, constructed
1911 to 1914.

pus. In 1929, and again in 1968, significant building projects joined the structures. The buildings were enveloped with yellow brick and capped with copper
overhanging eaves.[9] Neoclassical porticoes were added in 1929. When completed,
the units were known as Wards B and C and stood five stories tall, with four
floors of patient wards.[10] Each had a similar floor plan of a long ward with ancil-
lary rooms. The rooms on the north end of the ward included a reception area
for families, a consultation room, private rooms, a dining room, kitchenettes,
and baths. On the south end the floor plan terminated with a sunroom.[11]

   A 1914 Indianapolis newspaper article reported that the interior lighting was
remarkable. At the time, the Burdsal units were the only buildings west of New York
City to be lighted throughout with an innovative lighting system. Professionals from
other cities visited to study the system, with Cincinnati planning to model its hospital after the Burdsal pattern.[12] Heralded for its modernity, the Burdsal units also
became exceptional examples of Indiana art.

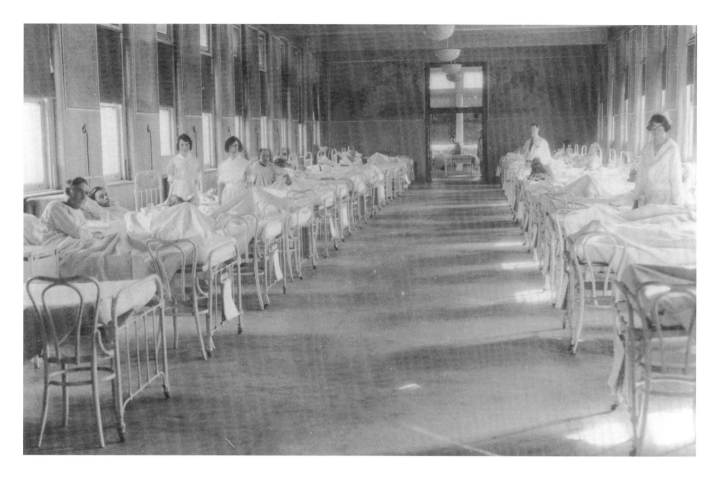

MILES OF WHITE WALLS

When they opened for patient care, the Burdsal units were extremely functional, but the decor was stark. There were literally miles of plain white wall space that beckoned for improvement.

Since 1907 City Hospital benefited from the St. Margaret's Hospital Guild, a ladies society that provided funding for special projects and supplies for patient needs. The Guild was named after a French princess who, according to legend, cared for children in her community. Supported by Dr. Lewis Brown, pastor of St. Paul's Episcopal Church, the Guild's mission was to care for sick children in the community. Originally children were treated at Eleanor Hospital on Capitol Avenue, but after it was destroyed by fire in 1909 children were cared for and treated in the basement of City Hospital. The completion of the Burdsal units allowed for better care of the pediatric patients as well as men and women. The ladies of the Guild took it upon themselves to beautify the new wards.

Representatives of the Guild approached Keene with an offer of two hundred

"Modern" interior of men's ward in the new Burdsal unit. William Edouard Scott painted the murals hanging on the walls.

The Art of Healing: The Wishard Art Collection

dollars for aesthetic improvements to the units. Keene concurred, stating later, "I wanted to do something valuable to the hospital and of some use as a memorial to the building itself and Mr. Burdsal."[13] Another account reports that the Guild's allocation was one thousand dollars.[14] "I told them that under no circumstances did I want to see the money spent for pots, kettles and pans or bed sheets or routine hospital equipment," said Keene. "These things the city could supply. I wanted these wards to be a little different from other wards. The $1,000 was the start of the idea."[15]

Keene happened to be a patron and a friend of many established and up-and-coming Indiana artists, so between the Guild and Keene the stage was set for a bold experiment. Keene had recently purchased a painting by Clifton Wheeler and conferred with him and another Indianapolis artist, Wayman Adams, to consider the Guild's offer. Instead of a few paintings, however, the artists suggested a large-scale mural project with the goal to create artworks for all of the wards in the Burdsal units.[16]

The money proposed for the project was not commensurate with the project's vision. Indiana's finest and most promising artists were invited to participate, except John E. Bundy of Richmond who was ill. Committed to the idea regardless of pay, the artists agreed to work for the wages of a union housepainter. This rate equaled approximately seventy-five dollars per month. Forsyth was designated as the general supervisor and earned one hundred and fifty dollars per month. In a 1940 newspaper article Keene stated: "Some of these younger artists were earning a rather precarious living, trying to live on what they could make or pay the rest of their way through school. A number were not so well established as they later became in life, and they welcomed a chance to earn even the comparatively low wages we were able to pay."[17]

In addition to the Guild's donation, the City Board of Health provided four hundred dollars for canvas and pigments.[18] In a further effort to defray costs, many of the artists moved into the unused Burdsal wards during the project and ate their meals from the hospital kitchens. Donations of money and supplies continued during the project, resulting in a total estimated at ten thousand dollars.[19]

The significance of this project is measured by the contributing artists and the scale of the work. In addition to Forsyth, Wheeler, and Wayman Adams, the remaining cadre was drawn from a pool of established and promising Indiana artists: T. C. Steele, J. Ottis Adams, Otto Stark, William Edouard Scott, Carl C.

Graf, Martinus Andersen, Simon Baus, Francis F. Brown, Jay H. Connaway, Helene Hibben, Walter Hixon Isnogle, Emma B. King, and Dorothy Morlan.[20] Once completed, their artwork covered a quarter mile of wall space, or thirty-three murals in many subdivided parts.[21]

The artists chose the rooms, hallways, and wards for their work, agreeing on soothing scenes and tones. The subject matter was at their discretion as long as the tone and style were complementary to the architectural designs.[22] As general supervisor, Forsyth selected a palette in muted tones. Because lead was known to react to the sulfa-rich environment created by coal-burning stoves and candlelight and would turn the paintings black, the pigments were mixed with zinc, which was more stable.[23] Forsyth's direction is apparent in Keene's recollection, "Forsyth laid down a rather broad panel or general scheme of colors for the project. The composition and execution, however, of the various murals were done in toto by the individual artists assigned to that part of the project."[24] These elements combined to create calming and healing scenery for early-twentieth-century patients.

For many of the artists, this was their first mural project. As a result, the murals

C-4 ward with William Forsyth murals.

were painted on sheets of high-grade canvas and then mounted to the walls using a mixture of white lead and damar varnish. This strong adhesive was secured further by covering the completed murals with heavy layers of varnish. While many of the artists painted on site, there were some exceptions. Steele painted his landscape murals in his Brown County studio, J. Ottis Adams in his Brookville studio, and Wayman Adams painted his portraits in his Indianapolis studio. Scott was the only artist to paint in situ, directly on the wall-mounted canvases.[25] The murals were hung on the upper half of the walls, above the eye level of an average man or woman, making the murals more visible to patients lying in bed.

THE ARTISTS

The gathering of artists at City Hospital was filled with a sense of dedication. Forsyth, Steele, Stark, and J. Ottis Adams's willingness to contribute to the project for meager compensation is evidence of that. Established as members of the Hoosier Group, these stellar artists often worked in the regionalist fashion, documenting the rich Indiana landscape in its many lights and shadows. Steele's City Hospital murals are indicative of the regionalist style. From this dedication grew camaraderie among the artists, especially those such as Scott, Graf, and Andersen, who lived in the hospital during the course of the project. This talented coterie enjoyed songs and an occasional opera from atop the scaffolding for hours at a time.[26]

The motivation for this artistic outpouring can be attributed to the project's public relations potential. In 1916 Forsyth wrote how public murals are the best ways "for art and the public to meet."[27] In addition, it was hoped by many that public displays such as this would lead to private commissions and other public works.[28] The City Hospital project also provided the opportunity to be part of something rare and unprecedented.[29] Presumably civic pride attracted many of the participants. The sixteen artists brought varied experience to the project. Forsyth and Steele were seasoned artists, and Scott and Wayman Adams were on the brink of greatness. The rest, although at the beginning of their careers, were already showing signs of great promise to their instructors.

T. C. STEELE

By 1914 Steele was a well-established member of the Hoosier Group and spent much of his time in his Brown County studio. He illuminated the women's surgical ward, B-1, with spectacular Brown County landscapes.

Steele was born near Gosport, Indiana, in 1847, but his family moved to Waveland when he was four years old. His artistic talent was encouraged while still young, and he received his earliest formal training at age twelve when he attended the Waveland Collegiate Institute, a college preparatory school. By age thirteen he was the school's drawing instructor. He continued at Waveland until he was twenty-one, and by 1870 he had arrived as a professional portrait painter. During that same year he married his favorite subject, Mary Elizabeth Lakin, who was his most supportive critic and love of his life until her untimely death in 1899.[30]

Settling in Indianapolis in 1873, Steele worked as a sign painter to make ends meet with his friend James Whitcomb Riley. The financial panic of 1873 found

Steele completed a total of eight murals, the focus of which were the four seasons: *Spring* (opposite page), *Summer*, *Autumn* (above), *Winter*.

(Previous page) *Autumn Landscape with Path.*

many aspiring and established artists looking for other sources of income.[31] In 1879 Steele's career took a new direction when he and his family moved to Munich, where he studied at the Royal Academy. Steele's European education was made possible by Indianapolis patrons, to whom he repaid with his canvases created abroad. Steele studied under Gyula (Julius) Benczur and Ludwig von Loefftz as did his friend and colleague Forsyth. Loefftz was his most demanding instructor, teaching him mastery of portraiture and figurative art. Outside of the classroom, Steele eagerly studied under landscape artist J. Frank Currier and developed a keen sense of outdoor light. Returning to Indianapolis in 1885, Steele arrived with great promise and the strong financial backing of many patrons.

The Steele family lived in Indianapolis at Tinker Place until 1901, when it was purchased and reopened as the first John Herron Art Institute. Summers were spent soaking up the landscape in various scenic locales. In 1898 Steele and J. Ottis Adams purchased a gorgeous home and property in Brookville, Indiana, which became known as the Hermitage. Adams lived there year-round, while Steele's family spent only the summers basking in the rich river valley and hillsides.

Steele married Selma Neubacher in 1907, the same year he purchased more than two hundred acres in Brown County, Indiana. The newlyweds set up housekeeping

in this remote hill county, and Steele entered the Brown County period of his career. Steele painted his murals for the City Hospital project in his Brown County studio.

In his City Hospital murals Steele depicted the Brown County countryside resplendent with seasonal color and light. He completed a total of eight murals, the focus of which were the four seasons: *Spring, Summer, Autumn, Winter.* They were displayed at the Herron Art Institute before their installation in the women's ward. Each season measured 60 inches by 111 inches and was too large for Steele's studio, requiring him to paint them in the living room of his house.[32] The series was described by Alfred M. Brooks in *The American Magazine of Art* in 1917. Brooks praised Steele's technique and interpretation, describing the seasons as "masterly and, decoratively, masterful. They bespeak the inherent bigness and breadth of the scenes they represent so faithfully."[33]

In addition to these masterpieces, Steele painted four vertical, narrow landscapes that adorned walls adjacent to the seasons that are equally stunning in tone and style. *Spring Trees* drips with the wetness of a plentiful spring and is the only vertical mural featuring springtime. The remaining three depict autumnal landscapes. *Autumn Landscape with Path* heralds the end of summer and the welcoming colors of fall. The viewer is encouraged to imagine walking the quiet

Steele also painted four vertical, narrow landscapes that adorned walls adjacent to the seasons. Two paintings named *Autumn Landscapes* frame views of the Brown County hillside in different light.

Steele depicted the Brown County countryside resplendent with seasonal color and light in his mural *Summer*.

path and taking in the surroundings. Two paintings named *Autumn Landscapes* frame views of the Brown County hillside in different light. One shows the turning leaves in rich red hues illuminated by late afternoon light, while the second features trees with yellowed leaves bathed in morning light. Steele's pastoral scenes were created to elicit a calming response from City Hospital patients and to soothe their psyche, thus empowering them to get well.

All of Steele's murals were salvaged in the late 1960s and removed from the ward walls. But the removal process was extremely damaging to the paintings, with several complex tears and excessive putty fill and overpainting. Of the entire Wishard Art Collection, however, the Steele murals remain the most striking and brilliant. A portion of the original eight hang in the Myers Auditorium, which is accessible to the public. One painting from the four seasons series, *Winter,* was given to the Indiana State Museum in 1976 in thanks for temporarily storing several paintings in the museum.

Steele's Brown County period progressed after the City Hospital project, and he produced some of his most memorable canvases. Steele's hospital murals are impressions of the Indiana landscape that he loved and are rich in technique. He continued to paint with the same passion until his death in 1926.

WILLIAM FORSYTH

Often referred to as the dean of Indiana art and artists, Forsyth was a member of the famous Hoosier Group and a longtime instructor at the John Herron Art Institute. In addition to serving as general supervisor of the City Hospital project, Forsyth left his work for generations of children to enjoy in the pediatric ward, C-4.[34]

Forsyth was born in California, Ohio, in 1854 and moved, as a teenager, with his family to Indianapolis. Forsyth demonstrated an early aptitude for art and attended the short-lived Indiana School of Art before studying abroad at the Royal Academy of Munich (1882–85), where artists Benczur and Loefftz influenced him.[35] Returning to the United States in 1888, Forsyth began his long career in education, teaching alongside his colleague J. Ottis Adams in Fort Wayne. Forsyth cofounded the Muncie Art School in 1889. Although the school was successful, he was attracted to city life and returned to Indianapolis in 1891. His teaching career continued alongside Steele at the Indiana School of Art until 1897 when it closed. That same year Forsyth married

one of his students, Alice Atkinson, and continued teaching private students and spending summers painting his beloved Indiana landscapes. In an effort to live among the scenery he adored, Forsyth moved his family in 1906 to the Indianapolis suburb of Irvington. Here with his growing family the artist enjoyed the rich colors of his garden and surroundings. It was during this time that he joined the faculty of the Herron Art Institute.

Although described as gruff and sarcastic, Forsyth is remembered as a remarkable teacher during his tenure as Herron's principal instructor in drawing and painting. One minute Forsyth would criticize a student's work and draw over it with charcoal to suggest how it should be done, and the next minute he would join his students for a smoke break on the back steps of the school. His demeanor as the general supervisor of the City Hospital murals is similarly remembered.

Selecting the palette and other criteria for the artists indicates a firm control of the mural project. On one occasion Forsyth criticized Graf's mistake in painting five fingers and no thumb on a figure, which was corrected. However, Forsyth made the same mistake on one of his figures that was never corrected.[36]

In addition to acting as general supervisor, Forsyth completed a series of murals in the Burdsal units. On C-4, originally the pediatric ward, Forsyth painted a series of children at play. On average the murals were eight feet tall and eighteen feet long. Unfortunately, many of the murals were damaged through the years due to a leaky roof. In addition to C-4, Forsyth painted a landscape for the main entrance hallway of the Burdsal units.

When several of the murals were removed from the walls in the late 1960s, Forsyth's series remained and was painted over. Only one painting, *Two Children*, exists as part of the present-day Wishard collection, and it was badly damaged when removed from the wall, resulting in several complex tears. In addition, heavy putty and overpaint was applied to the canvas creating a drastically altered appearance.[37] As of 2003 several murals remain in their original location on C-4, and all but one panel are covered with lime green paint. This section of the hospital is now known as BA 5 and is used for storage.

Forsyth commanded the canvas with strong brush strokes of light and dark, and his murals in City Hospital conveyed youthful energy through design and technique. Heralded for years through awards and competition, Forsyth spent the bulk of his career molding other Indiana artists. Forsyth died in 1935, two years after ending his teaching career at Herron.

Two Children was badly damaged when removed from the wall. In addition, heavy putty and overpaint was applied to the canvas creating a drastically altered appearance.

J. OTTIS ADAMS

Adams was the third member of the Hoosier Group to participate in the City Hospital mural project. His series of landscapes was created for the sunroom on B-1, the women's surgical unit.[38]

As a child, Adams saw much of the Indiana countryside as his parents moved frequently during his youth. Born in Amity, Indiana, in 1851, Adams completed his schooling in Martinsville. His artistic proclivity was apparent very early and was nurtured by his family and teachers. He pursued higher education at Wabash College but left after two years to develop his talents at the South Kensington School in London, England. It was during his studies in England that he developed his preference for landscapes by studying the works of John Constable and Joseph Mallord William Turner at London's National Gallery.[39]

Returning home in 1874, Adams supported himself by opening a portrait studio in Seymour and one later in Muncie. He returned to Europe in 1880 to study

Painted for the sunroom on B-1 of the Burdsal units, Adams's landscapes, *Whitewater at Brookville* (above) and *Hills and Seascape* (previous page) are a departure from his typical vibrant palette and composition.

at the Royal Academy in Munich, where many Hoosier painters were headed, including Steele, Samuel Richards, and, later, Forsyth. Adams and his colleagues studied under Benczur and Loefftz at the Royal Academy and informally with Currier. By 1887 Adams had returned to America and had begun teaching art classes. This led to the founding of the Muncie Art School in 1889 with Forsyth. After only two years the school closed, and Adams returned to private instruction. In 1894 Adams joined four other Indiana artists for a show in Chicago that created the name Hoosier Group and catapulted them into the mainstream art world. On the heels of this success and recognition, three of the group's artists, Steele, Forsyth, and Adams, cofounded the Society of Western Artists.

An avid outdoorsman, Adams found the ultimate landscapes in 1898 when he and Steele purchased the Butler house outside of Brookville. Known as the Hermitage, the summer retreat featured separate studio spaces on either end of the rambling house. In that same year Adams married artist Winifred Brady. Adams joined the faculty of the Herron Art Institute in 1902 and taught drawing and painting classes. But by 1905 Adams resigned to live year-round at the Hermitage with his wife and young family. It became the family's permanent residence when Steele sold his interest to Adams in 1907 and built his own studio in Brown County.

The family enjoyed cooler summers in Leland, Michigan, while Adams held summer classes at the Hermitage. Adams would join them for a portion of the time and relished the scenery. The Adams family enjoyed this idyllic lifestyle until a 1913 flood extensively damaged the Hermitage, requiring major repairs. That next year Adams joined his friends and colleagues for the City Hospital mural project.

The exact number of murals contributed by Adams is unknown. Two paintings are part of the Wishard art collection, *Whitewater at Brookville* and *Hills and Seascape,* but three walls of scenes from the Whitewater near Brookville were described in a 1940 newspaper article.[40] Painted for the sunroom on B-1 of the Burdsal units, Adams's landscapes are a departure from his typical vibrant palette and composition. These paintings are examples of the strictest adherence to Forsyth's predetermined palette with their muted tones and soft lines. Adams painted these at the Hermitage.

The following year Adams's health faltered, and he began spending the winters in Florida. His friend and fellow artist Stark often accompanied him on his travels to Indiana, Michigan, and Florida. During this time his catalog included the Florida landscape, where the light and textures inspired his work. Adams died in 1927.

OTTO STARK

*A*lthough not a single mural remains from Stark's artistic contributions at City Hospital, newspaper accounts report a dazzling toy mural painted for the sunroom of the pediatric ward on C-3. Stark was the fourth member of the Hoosier Group to participate in the mural project. The fifth member of the Hoosier Group, Richard B. Gruelle, did not participate as he was very ill and died before the project was completed.[41]

Born to a large German-American family in Indianapolis in 1859, Stark was apprenticed in the family tradition of cabinetmaking. However, his artistic instincts were strong, and he left woodworking to apprentice with a lithographer in Cincinnati. While there, Stark began exploring other artistic pursuits, including sculpture, painting, and drawing.

To hone his talents, Stark traveled to New York in 1879 and, six years later, the Académie Julian in Paris. Unlike his Hoosier Group colleagues, Stark studied under Gustave-Rodolphe-Clarence Boulanger, Jules-Joseph Lefebvre, and Fernand Cormon. In addition to developing his talents and signature style, Stark met and married Marie Nitschelm in Paris in 1886, and the couple soon began a family. After completing his studies, Stark returned to New York City in 1888, and his family continued to grow. After a later move to Philadelphia and the birth of their fourth child, Marie fell ill and died in 1891.

Supported by his extended family, Stark left his children in Indianapolis while he pursued lithographic work in Cincinnati. He returned to Indianapolis in 1893 and made a living by giving private instruction and exhibiting his own works. In 1899, to offset the financial demands of a large family, Stark took the position of supervisor of art at Emmerich Manual Training High School, where he influenced the careers of promising artists such as Scott. In 1902 he broadened his teaching career and began co-leading classes at the Herron Art Institute. This initial class led to his appointment in 1905 as instructor of composition and illustration.

During the next few years Stark found time to continue his own artistic pursuits and develop deep and enriching relationships with his fellow Hoosier Group artists. Spending time at Steele's Brown County studio and J. Ottis Adams's Hermitage, Stark enjoyed painting the Indiana landscape with his colleagues. He often traveled with Adams's family to Leland, Michigan, and spent considerable time at the Hermitage.

In 1913 Stark painted two large murals for Indianapolis Public School No. 60. This was his first work as a muralist. He later directed a team of artists in 1919 to paint a series of murals in five Indianapolis schools. That same year he retired from Manual and Herron.

Stark's City Hospital mural was created for the pediatric sunroom adjacent to the ward. Of the entire collection of murals, Stark's is the most joyous, featuring a collection of animated toys. The toys are romping in play and include a train, a bicycle, animals parading to the circus, toy soldiers, a baseball game, and more. There is even a king and queen of toy land presiding over the play against the backdrop of castellated turrets and towers. The only extant image of this mural is from a 1914 newspaper article.[42]

With his retirement, Stark was able to enjoy extended painting seasons in Leland and accompany Adams to New Smyrna, Florida, during the winter of 1920–21. On a smaller scale, he continued teaching his artistically talented granddaughter and volunteered as a Sunday school teacher at Roberts Park Methodist Episcopal Church. Stark died in 1926 ending a lifetime of sketching, painting, and teaching.

Eleven years after Stark's death a series of ten murals painted by Stark and Wheeler was donated to City Hospital. Originally commissioned by A. L. Block for the L. Strauss and Company store, the murals were donated to the St. Margaret's Hospital Guild for placement at City Hospital.[43] Intended for the children's ward, the murals depicted such Mother Goose nursery rhymes as *Rock-a-Bye Baby; Ding, Dong Bell; Simple Simon; Tom, Tom the Piper's Son; Mary, Mary Quite Contrary;*[44] *Pussy Cat, Pussy Cat, Where Have You Been?; Hark, Hark! The Dogs Do Bark; Jack Be Nimble, Jack Be Quick; Little Bo Beep* [*sic*]; and *Little Boy Blue*.[45] It is uncertain how many paintings ultimately were hung in the pediatric ward, but photographic evidence indicates that a number of them were placed in the occupational therapy clinic at the hospital.

WAYMAN ADAMS

As a portrait painter, Adams created one of the most endearing decorations for the Burdsal units, a series of twenty portraits of Indianapolis children. Designed for the pediatric ward on C-3, his was the only nonmural contribution to the project.

Hailing from Muncie, Indiana, Adams was born in 1883. His father, an artist himself who raised livestock and painted images of his horses on the walls of his barn, encouraged his son's considerable artistic talents. As a young boy, Adams was praised as a prodigy for his adept rendering of animal subjects and received his first commission. He began formal study at age twenty-one at the Herron Art Institute. During his four years of study, he developed his talents as a portrait painter and received commissions that helped pay for tuition.[46] His talents rose to a new level of skill after a trip to Italy with William Merritt Chase and a later trip in 1912 with Robert Henri to Spain. Returning to Indianapolis, he opened a studio and began a career painting portraits of Indiana governors, actors, and authors.[47]

City Hospital benefited greatly from Adams's skill at portraiture. The pediatric ward was of particular interest to the members of the St. Margaret's Hospital Guild, whose primary interest was in the care of sick children. With portraits of children on the walls, the Guild members hoped the patients might be comforted by familiar faces. Adams drew attention and excitement from the community as "beauty contests" were held to find the appropriate models for this project. Adams wanted a cross section of Indianapolis's ethnic population and socioeconomic groups.

Hopeful child models were seen at the Foreigners' House, the South Side Jewish Federation, the South Side Turners' Hall, at Germania Park, and the Colored Young Men's Christian Association. The models chosen were to reflect the nationalities of children who received treatment at City Hospital. In addition, pediatric patients were to be put into beds opposite the face of another child of the same ethnicity.[48] Twenty-five portraits were painted, and twenty were installed in the ward. Many ethnicities were represented, including Romanian, Hungarian, Serbian, Italian, and French. Notably, African-American and Jewish children were represented alongside children of physicians and bankers. A complete list of the child models can be found in Appendix 3.

The portraits were painted in Adams's downtown studio. The canvases were adhered directly to the wall in the same manner as the large murals. The portraits were framed with rounded molding also adhered directly to the wall. Years after the mural project was complete, visitors came to the hospital to see the portraits of themselves and their friends. One child died not long after he was painted. Joseph Henry Ward died while his father was in service during World War I.[49]

In the 1950s the portraits were taken down because of the deterioration of the wall plaster.[50] During the conservation project of the late 1960s, they were laid down and adhered to Masonite. Complex tears, excessive putty fill, and overpainting are evident. Of the original twenty portraits, nine are in the Wishard collection, one is owned by the Indianapolis Museum of Art, and the whereabouts of the remaining ten are unknown.

Of the portraits in the Wishard collection, only one remains close to Adams's original concept. *Tener Reko* is an image of a five-year-old Hungarian girl clutching a doll in her hand. While her facial expression is innocent, it also betrays a sense of indignation. Perhaps the doll was used to placate her for the sitting, as

Twenty portraits of Indianapolis children, such as *Richard William Etter* (page 24) and *Mary Vissa* (opposite) adorned the walls of the pediatric ward on C-3.

Tener Reko (left), *Anna Marie Brodeur* (right), and *Portrait of a Child* (opposite page).

she is the only child model holding a toy. This is also the boldest color scheme of the collection. The remaining portraits are less vibrant and align with Forsyth's established palette.

During the same year of the City Hospital project, Adams was awarded the Thomas R. Proctor Prize from the National Academy of Design in New York for his portrait of the director of the Indianapolis Orchestra, Alexander Ernestinoff.[51] In 1918 Adams married Margaret Graham Borroughs, and the couple had one child, a boy nicknamed Snig. He was naturally Adams's favorite model and the subject of many paintings. Later in his career Adams moved to New York and during his final years moved to Austin, Texas, his wife's home-town. He died there in 1959.[52]

WILLIAM EDOUARD SCOTT

The murals created by Scott during the City Hospital project were the most ambitious. Scott was the only African-American artist to participate in the City Hospital project, one of his many firsts. He concentrated on biblical scenes but also included a few pastoral and allegorical murals filling two wards, B-4 and C-1. As one of the first black artists to work professionally, Scott was a pioneer in African-American art.[53]

Born in 1884, Scott attended Emmerich Manual Training High School and studied with Stark, who was chairman of the art department. Stark regarded Scott as a talented student and encouraged him to study at the Art Institute of Chicago. Scott earned money for tuition as an assistant teacher at Manual, which gave him the opportunity to continue under Stark's tutelage. In this teaching role, Scott became the first African-American teacher in the Indianapolis school system.[54] With his savings, Scott enrolled at the Art Institute in 1904 and paid

A side room on C-1 show-
cased a Thanksgiving
scene, the "Pilgrim
Fathers." (above)

A series of murals
documenting the life of
Christ was created for the
women's medical ward.
Simeon and the Babe Jesus
(previous page)

for his five years of study through commissions. It was during this period that he completed several murals for the Chicago and Washington, D.C., public schools. He returned to Indianapolis in 1909 to save money for study in Europe.

Between 1909 and 1914 Scott took three trips to France, studying at the Académie Julian and later the Colorassi Academy. Scott's greatest influence while in France was Henry Ossawa Tanner, who provided food as well as artistic inspiration to the developing artist.[55] Much of Scott's technique and tone can be attributed to Tanner's influence.

Scott returned from his second trip to France in 1912 with several impressionistic pieces in tow and exhibited them in Stark's gallery. His talents were rewarded critically and financially through this show. In 1913 Scott was commissioned to paint murals for the Indianapolis public schools and was praised for his integration of classic compositions and themes, such as the "Old Woman and the Shoe," with African-American subjects. Scott became one of the first African-American artists to devote his career to depicting the black community's experience. Scott's purpose in capturing scenes of everyday life in the black community and portraying significant black figures such as Frederick Douglass, Booker T. Washington, and George Washington Carver was to engender an awareness of the black community, not act as an instrument of social protest.[56]

The Burdsal commission was completed as Scott's career was beginning to soar. In 1915 Scott spent five months painting several areas in the units. When completed, Scott's murals featured twenty-two panels and three hundred figures.[57] Perhaps influenced by Tanner, Scott created a magnificent series of murals documenting the life of Christ for the women's medical ward, B-4.[58] The main ward depicts: *The Boy Christ*, the *Three Magi and the Star in the East, The Nativity, Simeon and the Babe Jesus, Christ as Carpenter, Flight into Egypt*, and *Christ in the Temple with Elders*. In the lobby Scott explored other religious themes with the *Expulsion from the Garden of Eden*, the *Annunciation of Mary*, and on three narrow panels Moses, John, and Paul.[59] Scott also portrayed the women of the Old and New Testament in two forty-foot panels located on the upper portion of the walls.[60] Continuing down the corridor and into the sunroom, Scott illustrated the teachings of Christ. The corridor panels were titled *Suffer the Little Children to Come Unto Me* and *He Who Is without Sin*. The teaching series was completed in the sunroom with the works *Zacharias in the Tree*, the *Sermon on the Mount, Christ before Pilate, Christ Appearing to Mary after the Resurrection*, and *The Triumphant Entrance into Jerusalem*.[61] One account states that Scott painted himself as a robed Bedouin in the *Sermon on the Mount*.[62]

In his essay, "The Mural Tradition," Edmund Barry Gaither posits that these biblical scenes were meant to emphasize "practical and spiritual ideas about the central place of children in society." In particular he discusses *Christ with Simeon (Simeon and the Babe Jesus)* as a representation of the blessings of children.[63] Joseph and Mary are present in this composition, quietly providing caged doves as an offering. The baby Jesus looks straight at the viewer personifying health and youth with his full head of hair and sanguine expression. Thurman B. Rice's 1948 article, "History of the Medical Campus Chapter XXII: The Mural Paintings at General Hospital," however, suggests that B-4 was originally intended to be the mortuary and chapel, hence the religious-themed murals.[64]

Only one of the biblical panels survives today, *Simeon and the Babe Jesus*.[65] It was reported in 1913 by the *Indianapolis Star* that the Christ child was modeled after Weir Stuart, son of Dr. William Weir Stuart, a prominent African American and patron of Scott's. Florence Martin, nurse supervisor, posed as Mary.[66] In 2003 the Indianapolis Museum of Art conservation laboratory treated this painting, and the painting as well as the conservation process is featured in the *Art of Healing* exhibition.

Scott decorated a second area of the Burdsal units, and it is the least documented of his City Hospital contribution. On C-1, the lobby, corridor, ward, and sunroom were covered with Scott's murals. The lobby featured figurative work, and a side room showcased the "Pilgrim fathers,"[67] in which many of the hospital's nursing staff were used as models for a Thanksgiving scene.[68] The subject matter in the corridor is unknown. They were destroyed before Rice's 1948 assessment that documented the existing murals. In the men's ward area, Scott completed pastoral scenes that were badly damaged prior to 1948. Finally, a series of murals in the sunroom portrayed the "races of mankind."[69] The series was titled *The Nations of the Earth Coming to the Light.*[70] Three of these exist today, all of them from the pilgrim series, and are in the Wishard Art Collection.

Because he had worked as a muralist before the City Hospital project, Scott was comfortable working on a large scale. Unlike the other artists who completed their pieces on canvas and then mounted them to the wall, Scott painted directly onto the prepared canvas using scaffolds to reach high places. His palette has been described as having a silvery tone.[71] Another account describes many of the murals as faded; rather, this is in deference to the subdued tones and palette that Forsyth mandated.[72]

After his City Hospital experience, Scott's career and talent continued to develop, garnering praise along the way. In 1931 Scott received a Julius Rosenwald Fellowship to work in Haiti and spent a year capturing peasant life on canvas. His work can be credited with imparting an awareness of local scenery as worthy subject matter. Scott's influence and accomplishments in Haiti eventually led to a surge in interest in Haitian art in the 1950s and 1960s.[73] Scott painted within the realist tradition and maintained that perspective until his death in 1964.

CARL C. GRAF

A muralist since his late teens, Graf was a student of Forsyth's when he participated in the City Hospital project and just beginning to taste the professional artist's lifestyle.[74]

Graf was born in Bedford, Indiana, in 1892 and worked for the *Bedford Daily Democrat* after high school. While there, his sketching talents were discovered, and he began cartooning for the paper. Graf enrolled at the Herron Art Institute with the intention of becoming a cartoonist.[75] Instead, he studied portrait painting and sculpture.[76]

In 1914 Graf became involved with the City Hospital project. Quoted by a reporter in 1940, Graf reflected, "It was one of the most interesting experiments I've ever enjoyed. Many of us lived in the hospital—I stayed there 13 months—while the work was going on. It was one of those projects with no strings attached. There was some great work done there."[77] Graf's murals included landscapes,

classical figures, and fairy tales. They were painted in two areas of the Burdsal units, ward B-3 and the lobby and hallway on C-3.[78] When the Burdsal units opened, B-3 was reserved for the African-American women's surgical, medical, and obstetrical ward. C-3 was the pediatric floor.[79]

Most of the student participants had not dealt with mural work before. Presumably as a result of his previous experience, Graf supervised the installation of the murals. The artists painted on a heavy canvas that was adhered to the wall using a "mixture of white lead and damar varnish."[80]

For the African-American ward, Graf depicted a series of classical female figures, an example of which still exists in the Wishard collection. *The Three Women* has also been referred to as *The Three Muses* and is a portion of a larger composition. Its tone is muted in hues of pink, yellow, and blue. Rice noted in 1948 that canvases on the side walls of the wards had been seriously damaged.[81] In contrast to his figurative work, Graf completed a series of landscapes for the hall and sunroom adjacent to the B-3 ward. Only a portion of this series exists as well. It is an idealized landscape, strictly adhering to Forsyth's palette, utilizing soft yellows, greens, and blues.

Not to be outdone by Stark's parade of toys, Graf created a series of seven panels illustrating the Cinderella story. These hung in the lobby adjacent to the C-3 pediatric ward and were six feet tall. The panels progressed in this order: Cinderella worrying over her troubles, Cinderella forced to work, Cinderella receiving an invitation to the ball with the help of birds, Prince Charming at the party, the prince finding the slipper, the prince finding Cinderella, and Cinderella and the prince returning to the castle.[82] Graf's model for Prince Charming was a well-known handsome man himself, Dr. David H. Sluss, whose father, Dr. John W. Sluss, was a bone specialist at the hospital. David became a City Hospital staff physician but denied his resemblance to Prince Charming, depicted with flowing blond hair and an elaborate costume, for many years.[83]

In the hallway to the pediatric ward Graf painted a second fairy tale, *Elfin Grove*. The images tell the story of how the four seasons were created.[84] Both *Cinderella* and *Elfin Grove* are missing; most likely they were not salvaged from the walls during the late-1960s remodeling.

Once the murals were completed, Graf left for the East and studied at the Academy of Fine Arts in Philadelphia and at the Art Students League of New York. Before opening a studio in Indianapolis, Graf also studied at the

Graf depicted a series of classical female figures for the African-American ward. *The Three Women* has also been referred to as *The Three Muses* (opposite page).

Although Graf made pro-longed painting trips to Brown County to paint the lush Hoosier landscape, he painted idealized land-scapes for the Burdsal units. *Landscape* (above).

Cincinnati Academy of Art. He made prolonged painting trips to Brown County to paint the lush Hoosier landscape and won several awards at early Hoosier Salons. Graf married Genevieve Goth, sister of Brown County artist Marie Goth, and settled into the Brown County lifestyle.

Graf garnered his greatest accolades as a member of the Brown County artist colony and a founding member of the Brown County Art Gallery Association. He continued to accept sculpting commissions, but landscape painting was his passion. Graf died in 1947 at the age of fifty-four.[85]

CLIFTON WHEELER

*W*heeler was just finishing his formal education and on the brink of a remarkable career when he joined the City Hospital project. His contributions were sizable with a series of idealized landscapes in the men's medical ward on C-2 and the adjacent lobby and hallway. In the nearby sunroom he created farmland scenery, and for the sunroom off of the C-3 pediatric ward he illustrated a series of children's stories.[86]

Wheeler was born in the central Indiana town of Hadley in 1883. As a young boy his family moved to Mooresville.[87] His talents were apparent early, and he began his formal education as a private student of Forsyth, who took him on sketching trips into the Indiana countryside.[88] In 1902 Wheeler enrolled at the New York School of Art and studied with Chase, Henri, and Kenneth Hayes Miller. His fellow students and friends became celebrated American artists such as Edward Hopper and Rockwell Kent.[89] In 1907 and 1910 Wheeler traveled to

Europe with Chase's classes to study the Old Masters. During his second trip he met his future wife, the young artist Hilah Drake, who was the daughter of Alexander W. Drake, art editor of *Century Magazine*.[90]

Before his second trip with Chase, Wheeler began teaching painting and drawing at the Herron Art Institute, remaining a Herron instructor until 1933.[91] Soon after their marriage, he and his wife moved to Irvington, where his first instructor, Forsyth, lived and worked.[92]

Much of Wheeler's technique favored the impressionistic approach, the result of Forsyth's tutelage. But intermittently during his career his compositions are less of this manner and take on more bold and blocky forms and shapes. Both styles are found in the Wishard collection.

Women and Children is a portion of a much larger mural piece that filled one corner of the lobby on C-2. Created in an impressionistic manner full of quick and bold brush strokes, the paintings originally showed men, women, and children enjoying an idealized park setting. Other landscapes that filled the ward and adjacent hallway were idealized as well, but the artist's original technique is marred by conservation work done in the late 1960s. Although the landscapes presumably were created in the same impressionistic fashion, heavy overpainting obscures the original intent.

Wheeler joined Stark and Graf in creating fairy tales for the pediatric rooms. In the sunroom the Mother Goose stories of *Jack and the Beanstalk, The Goose Girl, Little Red Riding Hood,* and the *Pied Piper of Hamlin* came to life.[93] A reporter described the latter in 1914: "The naive simplicity of drawing and color in the fleeing figures, of quaintly frocked children, following the red-cloaked piper is a real joy."[94] A photograph of *The Goose Girl* was published in the same article and demonstrates that Wheeler's Mother Goose series was illustrative in nature using clear lines and color. Due to damage, Wheeler retouched the series in 1933 and 1947, but no evidence of these paintings remains today.[95]

In 1937 the fairy-tale theme was continued in murals by Wheeler and Stark that were donated to the hospital. Wheeler attended the January 1937 presentation of the murals by the St. Margaret's Hospital Guild at the hospital.[96] Painted on Upson board, the murals were placed in the pediatric ward and the occupational therapy clinic.[97] Their present location is unknown, and they are presumed to have been destroyed. In 1974, however, Hilah Wheeler Remaily, Wheeler's daughter, presented the hospital a series of watercolor cartoons that were the

Women and Children (opposite page) was created in an impressionistic manner full of quick and bold brush strokes.

Idealized Landscape by
Wheeler.

sketches for Wheeler's larger murals. The top right sketch became one of the occupational therapy murals, but the remaining sketches were not photographically documented, and their location is unknown.

Two years after his work at City Hospital, Wheeler painted the mural over the Circle Theater marquee on Monument Circle in Indianapolis. He depicted a classical scene of Grecian dancers on the outside and completed smaller figures inside the theater.[98] This composition and style are similar to his Mother Goose murals.

In 1933 Wheeler began teaching in the art department at Shortridge High School and spent his summers traveling across the country, painting the Rocky Mountains, the Catskill Mountains, the Smoky Mountains, and the Black Mountains of North Carolina. Always included in his repertoire were numerous landscapes of the Indiana countryside. Wheeler was a consummate artist who painted and sketched until his death in 1953.[99]

Original watercolor sketches for four of Wheeler's Mother Goose murals (above).

Martinus Andersen

MARTINUS ANDERSEN

Born in Peru, Indiana, in 1878, Andersen attended the Herron Art Institute and was a student of Forsyth and J. Ottis Adams. His idealized landscapes graced the corridor, lobby, and side rooms of the women's surgical ward, B-1, at City Hospital.[100]

During the project Andersen worked full time but managed to participate by moving into City Hospital and painting during the early mornings and by artificial light at night.[101] The scope of his contribution is unknown, but three of his large mural segments remain in the Wishard collection. Mary Q. Burnet described Andersen's work in 1921: "His murals in the Indianapolis City Hospital are individual and purely decorative, handled in masses broken with short brush strokes of color."[102] Another account of his hospital murals describes them as European in style: "Mr. Anderson's [sic] color scheme is attractively balanced in the masses devoted to lakes, forest, clouds, and the 'spotting in' of birds."[103] Unfortunately, excessive overpainting and putty fill have caused Andersen's murals to be some of the most damaged ones in the collection.

Simon Baus

SIMON BAUS

Born in 1882, Baus studied with Stark as a high school student at Indianapolis's Emmerich Manual Training High School.[104] He continued his studies at the Herron Art Institute, working with Stark, Forsyth, and J. Ottis Adams. Baus worked as a post-office clerk and painted portraits and landscapes in his off hours. He was also a member of the Irvington Group, which included Forsyth, Wheeler, and Helene Hibben, artists who painted and lived in the Indianapolis suburb.[105] Burnet described Baus's painting style in 1921: "His work is spontaneous and pleasing, a sympathetic interpretation of personality. In landscape he paints with a broad brush, in a high key, producing a brilliancy and rendition of . . . lights and shades."[106] Baus, like Andersen, had a full-time job during the project but managed to complete murals for the reception room on B-3, illustrating harmony in nature with landscapes of woods and lakes interconnected with pathways.[107]

Andersen's *Idealized Landscape* (opposite page) was part of a series that hung in the corridor, lobby, and side rooms of the women's surgical ward.

FRANCIS F. BROWN

Brown's first formal education was as a private student of J. Ottis Adams at the Hermitage. As a student at Herron, Brown participated in the City Hospital mural project,[108] painting a series of landscapes for the lobby of the African-American

Francis F. Brown

women's unit on B-3.[109] One large landscape remains today as part of the Wishard collection. It reflects the impressionistic influence of Forsyth and Adams. Brown was born in Glassboro, New Jersey, in 1891, but his family moved to Muncie, Indiana, when he was young. Brown received additional education at Earlham College, Ball State University, and Ohio State University.[110] He returned to Muncie and in 1925 became an art professor at Ball State, where he remained for thirty-two years.

JAY H. CONNAWAY

Connaway participated in the 1914 mural project, and two of his paintings survive today. Their original location in the Burdsal units, however, is unknown. It is likely that Connaway had just finished his formal education at the Art Students League of New York when he joined the project. In New York he studied with George Bridgman and Chase from 1911 to 1913.[111] There is no record as to whether he painted on site or if he shipped his paintings to the hospital.

Born in Liberty, Indiana, in 1893, Connaway was destined for a life by the sea. Before claiming the ocean as his muse, Connaway served in the army in World War I and found a strange avenue for his artistic talents. While at Base Hospital 32 in France, he drew colored drawings of the lesions on dead soldiers' lungs

Two *Landscapes* by Jay H. Connaway (below and opposite page)

caused by mustard gas. Although gruesome, this experience led him to the Académie Julian, where he studied with Jean-Paul Laurens, and later at L'Ecole des Beaux Arts. Connaway was the only artist in the City Hospital group to study at the exclusive institute.[112] Connaway spent seventeen years of his career painting on Mohegan Island, Maine, and then later in Vermont. He conducted the Connaway Art School during the summer months. Critics compared him to Winslow Homer because of his mastery of seascapes.[113]

Jay H. Connaway

In 1967 Connaway's City Hospital paintings were found after a prolonged absence. Two paintings that were presumed lost were found in a storeroom during remodeling.[114] Rice included Connaway in his list of artists in 1948 but does not describe the original location of his paintings.[115] The two "found" landscapes are wholly different from the types of landscapes Connaway typically painted. They were painted, however, before he lived beside the sea. Both pieces are of the same tone and similar composition depicting a quiet landscape.

HELENE HIBBEN

Hibben is often overlooked when discussing the City Hospital project. As the only artist devoted to sculpture, Hibben designed the sizable dedication plaque

Helene Hibben

for the Burdsal units. The bas-relief bronze tablet measured three feet by eight feet and was designed to hang above the door to the units.

Hibben was an Indianapolis native, born in 1882. She was a student of Forsyth, Lorado Taft, and James Earle Fraser. The latter two were her mentors while she studied at the Art Students League of New York. She was also a neighbor of Forsyth, living in the Indianapolis suburb of Irvington. The majority of her career was spent teaching youth art classes, first at Herron and then in her own school in Irvington.[116]

The bronze plaque was skillfully molded to depict classically draped figures, posed to the left and right of the inscription. The text is a dedication to Alfred Burdsal and was scripted by Hoosier novelist Meredith Nicholson. The bas-relief figures represent *The Spirit of Giving* and *The Recipients*. The Burdsal units were dedicated on 28 November 1914, with Mrs. Burdsal in attendance.[117] Today the plaque hangs outside the second-floor entrance to the BA building.

WALTER HIXON ISNOGLE

Walter Hixon Isnogle

Very little information has been published about Isnogle, but his mural participation at City Hospital is widely documented. Born in New Castle, Indiana, Isnogle studied at Herron.[118] He was regarded as one of the exceptional talents on the mural project and was one of the youngest artists to participate. According to a 1940 newspaper article, Isnogle's talents bred professional envy, and the other project artists often teased him. In return, Isnogle incorporated Graf's visage into a mural showing a man carving heads in stone. Graf's face was the subject being carved. For a while after the project Graf was nicknamed "Stonehead."[119]

Isnogle selected the theme of *Music, Literature, and Art* for his mural work, which was in the side room of the men's surgical ward.[120] When describing his City Hospital mural, Burnet raved, "His strong feelings for line and design has led him to place his figures, singly or in groups, with splendid freedom."[121] Isnogle's murals did not survive the various hospital renovations and are not part of the Wishard collection.

EMMA B. KING

King was a poet as well as an artist. She began her studies with Jacob Cox and later studied at the Art Students League of New York. Before beginning her studies at the Académie Julian in Paris, she studied with Chase at his Long Island summer school. She studied under Boulanger, Lefebvre, and Kenyon Cox while in Paris. As a world traveler, her canvases included a wide range of subject matter, including still lifes, seascapes, landscapes, and portraits.[122]

Painting for a private patient room on B-3 of City Hospital, King's murals were titled *Hope* and *Hope Fulfilled*. In cheerful tones King illustrated a quiet pastoral setting of houses sheltered by rolling hills, with the ocean serving as a background for the figure of a woman waiting for a boat to return home. The second mural, *Hope Fulfilled,* finds the woman's wish coming true.[123] King's murals have been lost.

Emma B. King

DOROTHY MORLAN

Morlan's talents were developed early under the guidance of her artist father, Albert Morlan. In addition to his instruction, she enrolled at Herron and learned from J. Ottis Adams and Forsyth. She continued her studies at the Pennsylvania Academy of Fine Arts in Philadelphia and the Henri School in New York. Like King, Morlan was a traveler who enjoyed painting a variety of landscapes and seascapes.[124]

Morlan's City Hospital murals for the side room and sunroom of the women's medical ward have not survived.[125] In 1914 Rena Tucker Kohlmann described Morlan's murals as "one of the most pleasing results in the line of pure landscape decoration in the entire set of decorations, in point of simplicity and restfulness in color and line. Bare trees and dark evergreen trees in masses are silhouettes against shades of soft cream, tan and green rolling country and placid gray water under quiet skies."[126] Some of the mural canvases had been removed from the walls by 1948, and many of those that remained were badly damaged.[127] One of these murals was salvaged, but its current location is unknown and only a photograph of it remains in the Wishard archives.

Dorothy Morlan

Francis F. Brown painted a series of landscapes, such as *Idealized Landscape* (opposite) for the lobby of the African-American women's unit.

AFTER THE ARTISTS LEFT

On 28 November 1914 the public was given the opportunity to see the murals before patient beds were moved onto the wards. Although artists were still working in the building, several wards had been completed. A reception was held in the units to showcase the murals and to acknowledge publicly Alfred Burdsal's bequest to the city. His widow was scheduled to attend as well as representatives of St. Margaret's Hospital Guild and the mayor.[128]

At the time, the participating artists felt that they had done some of their best work. Scott noted in 1915 that his work at the City Hospital was "the best bit of mural painting he [had] ever done."[129] Forsyth commented in 1916, "Perhaps the best work ever done by most of these artists is to be found on these walls; and it is no exaggeration to say that it is a monument to their accomplishments as artists."[130]

The project received national attention as well. The renowned muralist Thomas Hart Benton traveled to Indianapolis to study the murals. Henri, mentor to many of the artists involved, traveled from New York for a viewing.[131] Steele's *Four Seasons* murals were discussed in Brooks's 1917 article about the artist. The article was primarily a treatise on the compelling nature of art and artists, using Steele as the prime example. By 1917 Brooks had most of Steele's career to refer to, but chose the *Four Seasons* as the centerpiece of his discussion: "They breathe the inmost spirit of each season . . . the reaction of a poet to the ceaseless yet quiet hum of a July noon; to the rustling blaze of October; to the stillness of winter; to the promise which the annual return of spring makes and keeps."[132]

Despite the initial excitement, the advent of World War I replaced the murals in the public's consciousness. In addition, there was limited access to the murals because of their location in the patient wards. The murals essentially languished at City Hospital for the next several decades. Holes were cut in many to allow doorways; others were painted over or damaged by roof leaks and misguided attempts at cleaning. In 1933 and 1947 Wheeler returned to C-2 and personally restored his murals. Before 1948 the idealized landscape murals by Morlan in the B-2 hallway were removed, but their current location is unknown. At the same time Scott's murals in the C-1 hallway were painted over because of excessive damage.[133] These murals were titled the *Morning* and *Evening* and were painted in lavender, green, and yellow hues. *Morning* is sym-

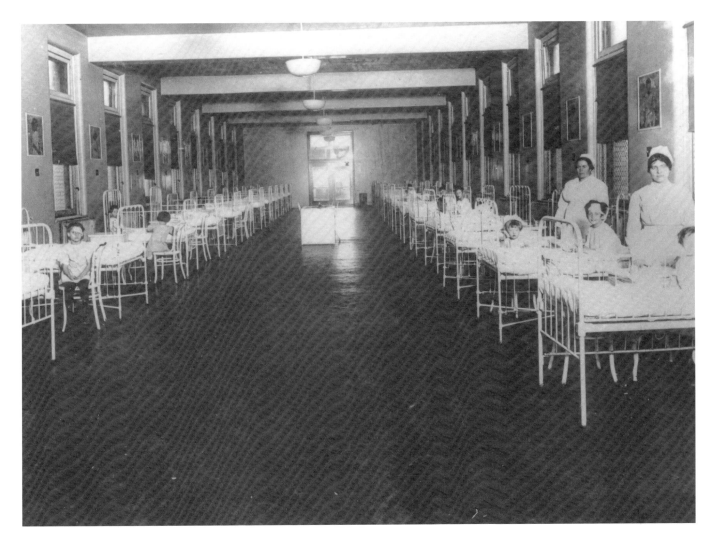

Pediatric ward on C-3 with Adams's portraits of children.

bolized by classically draped female figures casually preparing for the day against the backdrop of the morning sun. In *Evening*, the same figures are pulling their wraps around them as the moon rises behind them.[134] It is presumed that these murals were destroyed during the 1967 remodeling process, as they are not mentioned in later assessments.

In the 1950s Wayman Adams's portraits were removed from the pediatric ward because of deteriorating plaster. By 1957 the remaining murals were painted over except for eight Steele landscapes in B-1 ward, one Brown landscape in B-3 lobby, and the Wheeler landscapes in C-2 lobby and hall. By 1967 two to three more layers of paint were applied over the murals.[135]

Some of the observations made by the conservators from the Intermuseum Laboratory in 1967 described the location, size, construction, and condition of the murals. The laboratory's report specifically matched its observations with those published by Rice in 1948. With this assessment, several of the murals were prioritized for removal in 1967, when the Burdsal units were slated for remodeling.[136]

Although the level of damage to the murals was tremendous, blame cannot be assigned or attributed to any one factor. However, it can be noted that the daily operations in a hospital are often hectic and are focused on patient care. Murals such as these are easily taken for granted when human illness and trauma demand immediate attention. In addition, public facilities such as City Hospital experience a great deal of administrative turnover. Such inconsistency made taking proper care of the murals difficult. Also, the murals were sequestered in patient wards, which inhibited public viewing and led to an out of sight, out of mind situation.

The remodeling of the Burdsal units required extensive demolition, and the only alternative was to remove as many murals as financially possible. Once again, the St. Margaret's Hospital Guild stepped forward, initiating a "Save the Murals" campaign. Because of the hospital's public status, the salvaging and restoration of the murals could not be financed through the hospital's budget. Instead, the Guild solicited private donations and was successful in saving a portion of the murals.

The removal and conservation process, however, did not employ the best methods possible. Oversight responsibility for the mural removal is uncertain, except that Herron students were involved.[137] Several techniques for removal were recommended in the Intermuseum Laboratory's report, including using hand tools, solvents, water, and power tools, but the actual techniques used are unknown. Each painting, however, incurred serious complex tears during removal.[138]

The hospital retained a local conservation studio to conserve the paintings after their removal. Unfortunately, the methods used were not widely accepted techniques in the conservation field, and the paintings were further damaged. For example, putty was used excessively to fill in tears, creating an uneven surface. Extensive overpainting was also employed and not with an adept hand. Some areas of the paintings are so marred by overpainting that the artists' original intent is gone. Three of Wayman Adams's portraits were restored by Effie Carter, former Indianapolis Public School art teacher, but were actually repainted.[139] To make matters worse, oil paint was used, making the process nearly irreversible.[140] The majority of the collection was adhered to Masonite board to stabilize the canvas, causing further problems because the adhesive type and the composition of the Masonite is unknown.

A few of Adams's portraits were conserved by the Indianapolis Museum of Art in a proper fashion, but the bulk of the collection suffered a lesser fate. Once the work was completed, the collection was stored at the Indianapolis Museum of Art and the Indiana State Museum for a number of years. Finally, between 1975 and 1977, the collection was returned to the hospital, framed, and installed in various places, including the Myers Auditorium, physician offices, administrative offices, and conference rooms. Forty-three murals were salvaged from the walls,[141] and thirty-four were returned to the hospital. A number of pieces were given to the Indianapolis Museum of Art in gratitude for its services. In 1976 the Indiana State Museum was given Steele's *Winter*, which is part of the *Four Seasons*.[142] Unfortunately, this broke up the set.

For most of the next two and a half decades, the paintings remained in their installed locations. A 1977 fire in the Myers Auditorium caused water and smoke damage to twenty-four paintings, but they were returned to the hospital after being cleaned by Lyman Brothers.[143] From time to time the collection was insured and the inventory list updated, but they were generally left alone. In 1992 an independent conservator, Sharon D. Battista, completed a thorough condition assessment of the collection, but due to the lack of funds no action was taken to implement her recommendations.

Beginning in 1999, a new wave of interest in the collection developed surrounding the one hundred and fortieth anniversary of Wishard Health Services. The CEO and medical director, Dr. Randall Braddom, spearheaded efforts for the continued care of the collection. An updated appraisal was completed, a curator was appointed from the Wishard staff, and the collection was cataloged. As part of the anniversary celebration, the collection was exhibited during a special reception at the hospital.

The curatorial oversight of the collection has continued, and fund-raising for the conservation of the collection began in 2003. The IMA conservation lab is doing the work. The administration of Wishard Health Services and the Wishard Memorial Foundation are both committed to the continued stewardship of this remarkable collection.

THE WISHARD MURALS: DEMOCRACY ON CANVAS

Katherine C. Nagler

*I*n 1914, just as the golden age of Hoosier art was at its zenith, Indiana's leading artists embarked on an extraordinary public mural project at City Hospital (later Wishard Memorial Hospital) in Indianapolis that today is neglected and all but forgotten. Hailed in 1921 as "the greatest undertaking thus far in the art history of the state," these murals were the Hoosier version of the monumental mural style that swept America at the turn of the twentieth century. How that style developed and influenced Indiana painters is worth exploring, and the story of how the artists imbued this project with selfless, democratic spirit and idealism is a heartwarming vignette of Hoosier history and culture.[1]

The scale of the murals is as expansive as the artists' ambitions. To celebrate the opening of new wings at the hospital, the artists painted more than a quarter mile of murals and other works that not only decorated the new building but also, central to their artistic ambitions, lifted the spirits of the people inside.

While they painted, some artists even slept and ate at the hospital, while others sent canvases from their studios. Buoyed by the idealism of their shared enterprise and their artistic camaraderie, all, even the most famous, agreed to work for seventy-five to one hundred dollars a month, the going wage for union housepainters. No less an artist than William Forsyth directed the project, funded by the St. Margaret's Hospital Guild, and he enlisted others equally eminent: T. C. Steele, J. Ottis Adams, Otto Stark, William Edouard Scott, Wayman Adams, Carl C. Graf, and Clifton Wheeler, among others.

It is remarkable that some of the most renowned Hoosier painters even wanted to participate, for by 1914 Steele, J. Ottis Adams, Stark, and Forsyth enjoyed fine reputations and were well established. A single painting by Steele brought four thousand dollars. But as Forsyth wrote, "Nothing yet undertaken in the city has so roused the enthusiasm of our artists, for it was an opportunity to call out the best in them in a way not otherwise possible and realize something long dreamed of, but hardly hoped for."[2] Because the older and more established artists saw the murals as an opportunity to do something they had never had the chance to do, they embraced the project and invited the best of Indiana's younger artists to join them.

Although the established Hoosier painters had spent their careers painting in Indiana and were viewed by some as provincial, their accomplishments compare favorably to more famous East Coast artists. In the 1880s Steele, Forsyth, Stark, and J. Ottis Adams had studied in Europe, training that was de rigueur for American artists in the second half of the nineteenth century. Rather than settle on the East Coast upon their return, however, they came back to Indiana to celebrate the Hoosier land-scape. As one critic noted, "Mr. Steele learned in Europe only a better way of expressing Indiana."[3]

The mural project was the culmination of the unusual commitment to Indiana that Steele and the other artists demonstrated in many ways. By 1890, for example, these painters had opened art schools in Indiana, a measure of their dedication to providing an education to those who otherwise could not get one in the East or Europe. They continually made sacrifices—both personal and professional—to stimulate the arts in Indiana. Both Forsyth and J. Ottis Adams managed a strenuous weekly commute between their teaching posts at art schools in Muncie and Fort Wayne.

The artists' years of training and teaching, and their dedication to revealing Indiana's natural beauty on paper and canvas, peaked in 1893 when the Midwest took center stage at Chicago's World's Columbian Exposition. It is hardly an exaggeration to say that at the exposition the Midwest emerged as a major cultural force, and at its center were the artists of the Hoosier Group.[4] Critics and fellow artists celebrated the group's paintings, and Steele's reputation was particularly enhanced. The jury was reportedly quite surprised at the quality of his work. One said, "Mr. Steele's picture . . . is a beautiful one."[5] Not only were Steele's and Forsyth's paintings accepted against all odds for exhibition, but they were also prominently exhibited "on the line" in the Fine Arts building.[6] Also on display were murals painted for the exposition by such renowned artists as Mary Cassatt. It is possible that these murals, as well as the budding mural movement, kindled the ambitions that resulted in the City Hospital project some twenty years later.

The year 1893 was also important as the beginning of the art magazine *Modern Art,* the ambitious brainchild of Indianapolis designer and publisher Joseph M. Bowles. Inspired in part by the publications of William Morris, the English artist and a founder of the Arts and Crafts movement, *Modern Art* was, in the words of the eminent authority on American art, William H. Gerdts, "the finest, best-designed publication on art in this country."[7] The emphasis on design mirrored the publications of Morris's Kelmscott Press, which published finely crafted books that celebrated the traditional artistry Morris believed was threatened by industrialization and mass production.

Bowles began collecting Morris's books and used them as models for his magazine, intended as a "publication that showed 'the impress of as much art thought as any picture.'"[8] While Morris published the theories of English art critic John Ruskin, however, Bowles printed the ideas of Indiana artists Forsyth, J. Ottis Adams, and Steele. Gerdts asserts that many of the critically acclaimed essays that appeared in *Modern Art* were by the Hoosier Group on the subject of impressionism, including "The Evolution of Impressionism" written by Stark in 1895, and a treatise by Steele.[9] By the end of 1894 *Modern Art* could be found in the bookstores of sixteen American cities as well as in London, Paris, Leipzig, and Florence, and it had an international subscription list.[10] This unique Indiana magazine, along with the Hoosier Group's successful exhibitions and the force of their ideas, not only brought renown to Indiana's painters but also broadened their artistic ambitions.

After their success at the World's Columbian Exposition and an exhibition at the Denison Hotel in Indianapolis in 1894, Steele, Forsyth, J. Ottis Adams, and Stark were again invited to show their work in Chicago in 1895. Once again the critics raved, including the popular writer Hamlin Garland, an enthusiastic champion of impressionism. Garland promoted the idea of "nationalized modernism,"[11] which urged American painters to work within the impressionist aesthetic but to use American subject matter. The first and best regional school to accomplish "nationalized Impressionism" was Indiana's, which he celebrated as the Hoosier School, a name that stuck.[12] Seeing the works exhibited at the Denison Hotel and in Chicago, Garland wrote that even though the Hoosiers were isolated from fellow artists and surrounded by rather uninspired landscapes, they managed with their "uncompromising eye" to find "woods of color, graceful forms and interesting compositions everywhere."[13]

In spite of laboring in what Garland considered isolation, the Indiana artists continued to win international praise. Steele, for instance, received an honorable mention at the prestigious *Paris Exposition Universelle* of 1900. There his paintings were hung among works by James McNeill Whistler, Winslow Homer, and William Merritt Chase, further establishing an international reputation for him and for painters of the Indiana school. In 1910 Forsyth, J. Ottis Adams, Stark, and Steele all exhibited at the *Exposicion Internacional* in Buenos Aires, Argentina.

Considering their eminence and international laurels, it might seem surprising that Indiana artists embraced the chance to paint murals at City Hospital and to be paid almost nothing. Forsyth said this was an opportunity "the likes of which had never presented itself" to these artists. Looking back on the idealism of the project, Forsyth later wrote that the murals were "an opportunity to call out the best of them in a way not otherwise possible and to realize something long dreamed of."[14]

The mural project appealed to their artistic ambitions, to their strong sense of place, and to their civic spirit. It is possible the murals enticed them for other reasons, too. A new theory at the time held that a pleasing environment helped the sick get well faster, and that was among the reasons City Hospital's superintendent gave for promoting and funding the murals. Another popular theory held that children learned more in a pleasing academic environment, and so it is not surprising that many of the hospital mural artists also painted murals for Indianapolis Public Schools during the next decades.

Although public murals were new to America, they had ancient roots. Decoration of both public and private buildings is part of a long tradition in Western art. The frescoes of ancient Rome, the mosaics of the Middle Ages, and the great Renaissance decorations at the Vatican apartments, the Sistine Chapel, Florentine churches, and the palaces of Venice, are but a few of the best known. Forsyth may have had such examples in mind when, writing of the hospital project, he recalled the grand tradition in these words: "The decoration of walls in public and private buildings has always been the chief field of achievement in all the best periods of art and the field to which all artists turn when opportunity offers to express the best that is in them."[15]

Forsyth was also aware that grand murals had been added to many of America's finest buildings, and today the period called American Renaissance is known as the golden age of mural painting. An estimated four hundred public and private buildings were expansively decorated by famous artists, including such landmarks as Boston's Public Library and Trinity Church; the Church of the Ascension, Union League Club, and the Vanderbilt mansion in New York; Maine's Bowdoin College Art Gallery; state capitols in Minnesota, Wisconsin, and Iowa; the courthouse in Baltimore; the federal courthouse in Cleveland; and the U.S. Capitol and the Library of Congress in Washington, D.C.

American Renaissance was the dominant art and architectural style from the 1870s to the 1920s. Less nationalistic than the landscape school that had dominated American art before the Civil War, the new style emulated European culture and tradition. During the post–Civil War period of prosperity, wealthy industrialists and financiers began to see themselves as the counterparts to Europe's aristocracy. At the same time, advances in transportation made Europe more accessible, and those who could afford it increasingly traveled abroad, where they developed a taste for European grandeur and luxury. It is no surprise that their neo-Renaissance homes, whether in Newport or in Indianapolis, such as J. K. Lilly's house, Oldfields, were modeled on the villas of sixteenth-century Italian princes and the châteaux of seventeenth-century French nobility, and were often filled with European masterpieces.

The same neo-Renaissance style was promoted by the Ecole des Beaux Arts in Paris, a style embraced by many fine American architects, including Richard Morris Hunt, Stanford White, and Henry Hobson Richardson. Their beaux arts style gave countless clubs, libraries, train stations, and art museums the grandeur of Europe's golden ages. Intended to rival Europe's masterpieces, the buildings asserted America's internationalism, cosmopolitanism, and culture. Prosperity and a population boom that moved westward added demand for new governmental, religious, and social buildings, all increasingly based on European models. Such cultural currents swirled in Indianapolis, too, where notable beaux arts and neoclassical buildings built during the American Renaissance include Paul Philippe Cret's Indianapolis Public Library and John Herron School of Art, the statehouse (replacing an earlier building stiffly modeled on a Greek temple), the Soldiers and Sailors Monument, and City Hospital. And what could be more natural than to decorate these paeans to European culture with the same elements as found in the originals—stained glass, architectural sculpture, and murals?

Eager to compete with and learn from their European counterparts, American artists and architects studied abroad. Foreign study became not only a mark of sophistication but also a de facto requirement for important commissions. Among those influenced by their study at the Ecole des Beaux Arts were the leading New York City architects Hunt and Richardson, and the principals of the famous architectural firm of Charles F. McKim, William R. Mead, and White. It is no surprise, then, that artists from Indiana and Ohio also felt it was important to study abroad and to continue their involvement abroad, just as the Hoosier Group did, with exhibitions at important European juried exhibitions such as the Paris Salon.

Among the first notable murals of the period are those enriching the elaborate interiors of Richardson's Trinity Church in Boston. The artist, John La Farge, collaborated with Richardson from the outset and also designed some of Trinity's famous stained-glass windows. As influential as it was original in design, Trinity Church established Richardson as an American master and also showed how murals could enhance architecture. The confluence of similar ideas about architecture and painting can be traced in the careers of the famous Hunt brothers. Richard Morris Hunt, whose renowned buildings include the Metropolitan Museum and Biltmore House (the Vanderbilt home), studied at the Ecole des Beaux Arts, as did his brother, painter William Morris Hunt, who painted the murals in the New York Assembly Chamber. Murals in the buildings of this period increasingly were part of the original architectural conception. In contrast, the U.S. Capitol had murals painted as early as the 1820s. These were painted piecemeal, however, and did not carry a unified theme.

That La Farge and William Morris Hunt were pioneers in the American mural movement owes in part to their study in Paris, where they learned the European mural tradition in the 1840s and 1850s (although American artists had studied in Europe since the colonial period). La Farge assisted Thomas Couture, student of Eugene Delacroix, in decorating the Chapel of the Virgin in the Cathedral of St.-Eustache in Paris. The success of Trinity Church not only made Richardson and La Farge famous but also helped cause a boom in decorative-art projects. The boom took many forms. Artistic firms and societies were created, even in smaller cities, to promote the new movement in the decorative arts. The short-lived Arts and Crafts Society of Indianapolis included among its charter members Steele, J. Ottis Adams, Forsyth, and Stark, prominent muralists a decade later at City Hospital.[16] Across the country demand for historically based decorative styles exploded.

Critics of the period urged artists to consider all historic styles and movements for guidance, and although the Italian Renaissance was particularly cherished, medieval-inspired decoration also proved to be popular. The Renaissance style influenced not only architecture but also mundane arts such as greeting and Christmas cards, magazine graphics, wallpaper designs, stained glass, firebacks, and ceramic tiles. The most famous architectural firm of the period, McKim, Mead, and White, continued to promote mural decoration and invited the best American artists to paint murals in its buildings. Among these buildings were the firm's 1893 World's Columbian Exposition structures, all in the beaux arts style and featuring important and influential murals by such celebrated artists as Cassatt. Other artists included J. Alden Weir (a prominent American impressionist), Mary Fairchild MacMonnies, and Robert Reid. These murals, indebted to the style of decoration in the much admired Paris Opera, were an immediate inspiration for the whole mural movement in the United States.[17] Perhaps those murals influenced the Hoosier painters who attended the exposition; however, men as well traveled and conversant with trends as the Hoosier Group would have been aware that murals were becoming a signature element of important buildings.

Mural projects always require collaboration, ideally between the architect and the painters, but always among the painters themselves. The latter type of collaboration follows a long artistic tradition in which careful coordination is required to create a unified and harmonious work of art. Muralists in nineteenth-century America followed the same practice used during the Italian Renaissance in which a master artist worked with apprentices in his workshop. The master was responsible for the overall design and usually the formative parts of the mural, such as the cartoon design and the painting of the major subjects. Following the master's design, the assistants filled in the areas requiring less skill and performed the more tedious, repetitive work. Compared with this controlled and hierarchical arrangement, the scheme for the hospital murals was a free-for-all. Forsyth supervised the painting and laid out a general color scheme that was meant to be soothing to patients, but beyond that he allowed artists freedom to paint whatever they wanted. Giving young artists—some were only students—such freedom was a progressive idea that sprang from Forsyth's experience as a teacher. Certainly it bespoke his confidence in the artists, and it reinforced the sense of camaraderie and shared purpose, completing the sense of idealistic dedication from artists who slept, ate, and painted at the hospital. The young Wheeler later said that many of them did their finest work during the Wishard project.[18]

Forsyth also did not dictate the subject matter, again a significant difference from the usual practice. The project's guiding theme was simply to promote comfort for the sick. By eschewing complex allegorical and didactic subjects based in history, the Hoosier painters stepped outside the prevailing style, but in the atmosphere of freedom they painted what they knew, what they did best, and what they thought the patients and their families would most appreciate.

Steele, J. Ottis Adams, and Forsyth, the masters of landscape, painted Hoosier landscapes, while Stark and Wheeler painted whimsical nursery-rhyme illustrations that would appeal to ill children. Scott painted the religious paintings that became his major subject matter in the later murals that made him famous. In this style he was likely influenced by the famous African-American painter, Henry Ossawa Tanner, with whom Scott had studied in Paris. Wayman Adams, master of the portrait, filled the pediatric wards with portraits of children representing all the ethnic groups in Indianapolis, faces that would be comforting because they were familiar.

The Hoosier artists, buoyed by passion and skill and by their idealism and the confident belief that they were working in a thoroughly modern manner with ancient antecedents, painted a quarter mile of murals to bring comfort and healing. Although that was enough, there was more to this project, for another purpose—originating from the democratizing impulse of the Arts and Crafts movement—was to bring art out of the museums and drawing rooms of the wealthy and to put it before the public. "In a country such as ours with our form of government," wrote Forsyth, "it also seems the most natural and logical way for art and the public to meet on a common ground of understanding and appreciation."[19]

These murals, then, were not only paintings of familiar Hoosier faces and places but were democracy on canvas. In that same egalitarian spirit, Indiana's best artists gave artistic freedom to their less experienced colleagues. After all, had they not slept and eaten together as a band of brothers? And so it was "natural and logical" to place their palettes and their talents on the walls of a hospital dedicated to the poor and to find there "an opportunity to call out the best that was in them."[20]

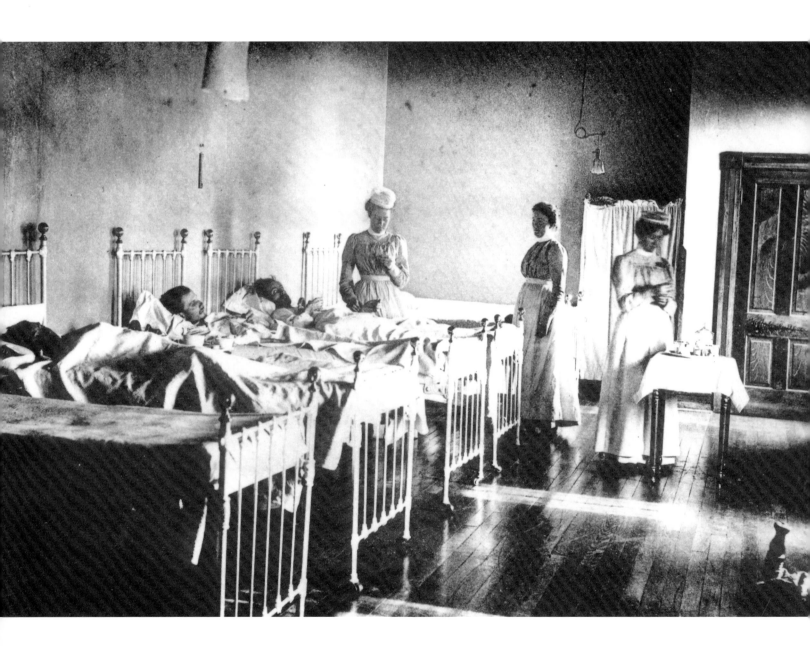

Early image of men's ward
at City Hospital before
Burdsal units, 1894.

CARING FOR THE COMMUNITY: THE HISTORY OF WISHARD HOSPITAL

Hester Anne Hale

Some 150 years have passed since the first petition for a city hospital gained enough support for a building to be mandated by the city council. And the way was not easy. From the outset, the hospital and its promoters were scoffed at and decried. Once it was built, no one wanted it. Many questioned how Indianapolis taxpayers could afford to maintain it and why they should want to.

The mission of the first hospital remains Wishard's primary one today: to furnish quality medical care for the indigent and be open to all residents of the city and county regardless of financial or social status. Through the years, that obligation has been foremost. Because of its dependence on tax support, the hospital has frequently come under fire. In earlier days local politics played a large part in hospital decisions and policies. As a city-owned hospital, its troubles and its successes were public matters. The community took an avid interest in what went on there.

Much of the progress in shaping the hospital grew out of the vision and energy of such men as Dr. William Niles Wishard and Dr. Charles W. Myers. Indianapolis medical colleges contributed to the education of the hospital's medical staff. Later, through its close association with the Indiana University School of Medicine, the hospital developed into an even stronger teaching institution.

THE MILITARY HOSPITAL, 1859–1866

The first Indianapolis city hospital was, in the opinion of many, a mistake that should have been avoided, draining a city treasury that could ill afford the cost of its construction and repair. For nearly three decades, the building of a city hospital had been a controversial issue. Begun in 1855, it was finally completed four years later. But by then no real need was seen for the building, and popular sentiment declared it a costly waste.

The *Indianapolis Sentinel* on 16 August 1859 pronounced it not only a useless building but also a public nuisance. Despite locked doors and fastened windows, vagabonds were taking possession of it. It was said to be a den of prostitution. "We have no need of a hospital, and if we had, the people in the neighborhood of the building would never permit it to be made the receptacle of malignant or contagious diseases," the *Sentinel* intoned, adding that the money could just as well have been sunk into the White River. On 13 December 1859 the *Sentinel* declared, "The hospital is a monument of Democratic folly, originating in the brain of Dr. [Livingston] Dunlap who, aside from his connection with this project, made a very fair councilman."

As a physician Dunlap deplored the conditions that allowed the spread of serious diseases such as malaria, smallpox, and cholera. He had been the chief advocate of a hospital that would provide treatment and care for the city's seriously ill, particularly those without the means to care for themselves. Dunlap began his crusade in the 1830s, and so strongly did he urge the building of a hospital that the project soon became known as "Dunlap's Folly."

Smallpox was greatly feared because often, before a case was diagnosed, the contagion was rampant. Only in the face of these epidemics did there seem to be a real concern for public health.

In 1848 a former Indiana congressman, Andrew Kennedy, in town on a visit, was staying at the Palmer House at Washington and Illinois Streets. Suddenly, he contracted smallpox and died. The disease spread. The city council was quick to call a public meeting. General vaccination, in the Board of Health's opinion, was the best means of controlling the disease. Emphasized, too, was the need for a special place for smallpox victims or victims of any other malignant disease, an idea that once again pointed to construction of a city hospital. The response from the public was positive, and resolutions were passed instructing the council to proceed.

The financial condition of the city government, however, was precarious. No funds were available because the city was already in debt several thousand dollars. Furthermore, a restrictive clause in the city's charter prevented the city council from raising funds for any cause beyond an amount sufficient to carry on city government. Encouraged by the positive response of townspeople attending the public meeting, the city petitioned the state legislature to have the charter amended, and the petition was successful.

A legislative act amended the city charter to permit defraying the expenses of any measure the council might adopt in order to prevent the spread of small-

Smallpox ambulance in service 1905 to 1908.

pox. The next step was to levy a special tax. Not all of the city's residents favored a hospital, or smallpox, tax. A hospital fund assessed by order of the council for smallpox purposes was a decided failure. By 1 May 1849 only $766.51 had been levied, and the council conceded that any attempts to collect the tax would prove fruitless.

In February 1854 the hospital issue came alive again. By this time Indianapolis had a population of twenty thousand, and Dunlap and Dr. John Bobbs addressed a petition to the city council once more urging the city to take action for housing the sick.

Dunlap asked that a committee of three be appointed to consider a site for the new hospital.

Finding the right setting for the hospital proved difficult. At each proposed site, neighbors raised objections, chiefly out of fear that the illnesses being treated there might endanger their health. The final choice was made in December when the council approved the purchase of eight acres situated on Fall Creek at what was then the end of Indiana Avenue. This property was considered remote and, because it was so near swamps, unhealthy.

In January 1855 smallpox broke out again in Indianapolis and contagion spread. The council once again acted promptly to control the disease by urging that all persons be vaccinated. The outbreak soon abated. The *Indianapolis Locomotive* commented: "The nine days wonder is over and the only consequence is an innumerable number of sore arms." But an even more important consequence was to follow—the building of the long-delayed hospital.

By 1857 the south wing of the hospital was raised to its expected height of three stories. Architecturally, the building was impressive. Constructed of brick, with limestone detailing, it could accommodate fifty patients. For the more progressive citizens, this hospital was yet another asset of the growing city of Indianapolis, which had developed rapidly as a seat of manufacture and commerce.

In 1859 the *Indianapolis Journal* commented that the hospital, which had cost $30,000 with some $2,000 still owing, was of no more use than "a lighthouse on the White River to protect the commerce of that stream." Later that year the *Sentinel* declared it to be "a fine looking edifice, fairly constructed, but of no use to anybody as it stands."

What, then, was the city to do with this hospital building and grounds? The outbreak of the Civil War answered that question. When Indiana troops were called up, Indianapolis became the center of military activity in the state. In May 1861 municipal authorities turned the hospital over to the state without charge. Gov. Oliver P. Morton offered the building to the federal government to be used as a military hospital. At last, the hospital building was to achieve its intended purpose.

One month after it was opened as a military hospital, a local journalist went there to find a story. He was pleased to find the building clean and well ventilated, and he was "astonished to find how thoroughly all the needs of the sick had been provided for in such a short time." In that first month, three hundred patients had been treated, with no fewer than fifty patients at a time, sometimes nearly one hundred. The hospital served the military until 1 July 1865, after which it reverted to the city of Indianapolis.

CITY HOSPITAL, 1866–1947

On 1 July 1866, Dr. Greenly V. Woollen opened City Hospital as a charity institution to be supported by the taxpayers. The only addition made to the hospital building was a small amphitheater for medical lectures. Woollen was a respected local physician and an excellent choice to oversee the hospital.

Woollen's task in summer 1866 was not only managing the new city hospital but also holding its expenses as low as possible. Few people recognized the difficulties that he and others working with him experienced. The average Indianapolis resident had little appreciation of this type of charity institution and perhaps even less understanding of the city's need for it.

Monetary problems continued to plague both the city and the hospital throughout the 1870s. Complicating these financial pressures were the prevalent attitudes toward poverty. People saw a distinction between paupers and the deserving poor, between those lazy persons too ready to accept charity and those persons whose disabilities, old age, or ill health prevented them from supporting themselves.

The city's low death rate was due more to fortuitous circumstances than to any true conception of public health. Sanitation conditions in the city in the 1870s were deplorable. It was not until 1875 that the city took any action about the collection of garbage. Stagnant ponds were found in many neighborhoods. There were no effective controls on waste disposal from manufacturing plants, and no more than 10 percent of private homes had indoor plumbing.

The next decade brought a new understanding of the importance of sanitation. The germ theory, as it was known, revolutionized medicine and at the same time gained the public's confidence that medicine could solve the problems of disease. It helped the medical profession gain greater respect and broke down the commonly held belief that hospitals were responsible for spreading diseases.

This new medical era predated by a short time the appointment of Dr. William Niles Wishard as superintendent of City Hospital. He was not quite twenty-eight years old when he took over the position in 1879. An 1874 graduate of the Indiana Medical College, he studied at Miami Medical College at Cincinnati for two years before returning to join his father, Dr. William H. Wishard, in the practice of medicine.

Wishard's term as superintendent from 1879 to 1887 nearly doubled the total years of the three men immediately preceding him. The hospital's "Wishard years" proved significant. Under his direction long overdue changes led to an improved City Hospital, both in terms of the physical plant and in management. When he began, the old brick-and-frame building was little changed, and in the ten lean years since the Civil War it had not been well maintained. Poor ventilation and warped, uneven floors were only a small part of the problem. Snow came in the windows and the roof leaked, causing patients on the third floor to be moved to dry areas and basins put out to catch the water. On rainy days the cook held an umbrella over his head while he prepared meals.

Reconstruction of the hospital's physical plant was one keystone of Wishard's administration. He secured the needed appropriations, planned the additional space, and oversaw construction for the three buildings erected from 1883 to 1885. Some have referred to this accomplishment as "Wishard's Wisdom," an improvement over the derisive term given to the hospital earlier "Dunlap's Folly."

Wishard showed the citizens of Indianapolis and the city government that he was a superintendent to take note of. While he was known to be understanding, sympathetic, patient, and fair, he was also respected as a self-disciplined, formidable, and highly ethical advocate for what he felt to be right. His foresight, good judgment, and tenacity was demonstrated by large three-story brick buildings going up on the old hospital grounds.

In 1883 with the Flower Mission, Wishard instituted a nursing school, the second such school west of the Alleghenies. (The Flower Mission, founded in 1892 by Alice Wright, was a private organization dedicated to providing services to the city's indigent.) More than just dutiful servants following the physician's directions, nurses were taught to observe and record what was taking place in the sickroom and to be efficient in emergencies.

Wishard was impressed by reports of the successes of a New York hospital's use of antiseptics in its obstetrics ward. He described for members of the

Marion County Medical Society results in the wards of his own hospital. During a fifteen-month period at the hospital, antiseptic methods were used. In more than seventy obstetrical cases during that time, no deaths occurred. Also, all of the so-called hospital odors disappeared, and wounds healed quickly. Prior to this, the mortality rate had ranged from 4 to 5 percent. Wishard believed that operating a hospital without antiseptics was criminal. In the very early days, surgeons washed their hands after operating, not before. In the operating room, they wore long coats to protect their clothing, not the patient.

Wishard was receptive to modern approaches to medicine and very much aware of work being done in other hospitals. Most of all, perhaps, he gave stability to the hospital and firmly fixed its place in the city.

During the 1890s six men served as the hospital's superintendent, five of them staying for a term of two years or less. These changes reflected the restrictions and demands that city politics placed on the hospital's management. Fortunately, the men appointed to the position of superintendent were well qualified, and the efficient management of the hospital was not seriously impaired.

Even though it did experience some instability from frequent changes in administration, City Hospital continued to expand. In 1895 the hospital broke the color barrier with the selection of an outstanding young man for its intern program. Samuel A. Furniss, an African American who graduated second in his class at the Medical College of Indiana, passed the

Ward B-1 with Steele's *Four Seasons*.

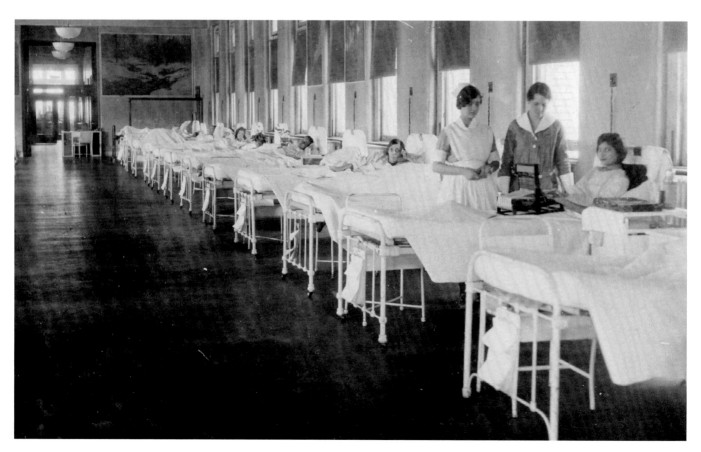

Board of Health examination with a high score. Noting that objections had been voiced in some quarters, a newspaper commented, "Dr. Furniss earned the position which has been given him, and all fair-minded people will insist on his having it. . . . If there are men or women in the hospital who feel they cannot serve with Dr. Furniss because his skin is a little darker than theirs, they can resign."

By the close of the nineteenth century, City Hospital appeared to be doing well. For thirty-four years it had provided medical service primarily to the indigent but to other patients as well. It had survived many crises and had weathered the upheavals in staff and the constant political squabbling.

In the pre–World War I years, City Hospital began a major construction project. The first major financial gift was made by Indianapolis businessman Alfred Burdsal. His large bequest made possible a modern addition to the hospital. This important gift and the art project that developed because of it were the big news of the new decade. In November 1914, two four-story isolation units were built near but not connected to the hospital. These Burdsal units later became known as B and C wings of the hospital. Two wards were reserved exclusively for children.

Two elements contributed to the Burdsal story. The first is St. Margaret's Hospital Guild. Formed by the pastor of St. Paul's Episcopal Church in 1907, the work of the Guild was dedicated to sick children. The Guild assumed responsibility for furnishing and decorating the new wards of the Burdsal unit. The second was Dr. T. Victor Keene, then president of the board of health. When St. Margaret's Hospital Guild approached him with money to be used to some purpose in the new units, the art project was born.

It was an exciting project, and the artists chosen were enthusiastic. Not only were they working on subjects familiar to them, but they were also enjoying the opportunity to join other artists at work. All of them had the same goal—to create walls of memorable art to interest and to delight the patients in the wards.

At the conclusion of many months of work, thirty-three different murals had been created—the work of well-established artists, younger artists, and local art students. Although the general public was certainly aware of the art project at the hospital, other events at the time took priority. Interest in the murals, Keene found, was eclipsed by news of the outbreak of war in Europe. Three years later, when the United States entered World War I, attention was focused on American military operations abroad.

Wartime restrictions had a great impact on City Hospital. Shortages in both personnel and general supplies greatly hampered the hospital's effort to care for its sick and injured patients. All expenses were rising. In 1918 Mayor Charles Jewett, making a tour of inspection of the hospital, was appalled at what he saw. He vowed that one of the key objectives of his administration would be to keep the hospital in the future from becoming "a football of politics."

The 1920s began in a spirit of optimism and confidence. The hardest years seemed to be over, and City Hospital began to grow. Among several innovations that proved very successful was the Social Service Department. The department served two purposes: to give attention to the social condition of a patient in order to improve and safeguard recovery and to try to relieve any factor that would retard the patient's response to medical treatment. This department grew rapidly. Financial investigations of patients were instituted and attempts made to screen patients who could pay for private medical care. The department brought other innovations to the hospital as well. In 1921 the Indianapolis Public Schools began a school for convalescing children, and later the Indianapolis Public Library opened a branch at the hospital.

The American Hospital Association's accreditation in 1925 brought a great honor to the hospital. In three years the hospital's rating from this organization had moved from Class C to Class A. This upgrading came as a result of deliberate efforts to match community needs. As well as adding new buildings and making other improvements in the physical plant, the hospital had expanded its services to provide care for more people.

In 1931, the hospital's sixty-fifth year, Dr. Charles W. Myers became its twenty-sixth superintendent and the man who would serve the longest term, working there until 1952. When asked what he felt his duties were as superintendent, he listed three: to look after patients to see that they received proper care, to see that the hospital was managed economically and efficiently, and to assist in all forms of research. The influence of Myers's management was significant. During his tenure City Hospital gained new respect in the community, public complaints about its shortcomings waned, and newly constructed buildings provided space to accommodate and efficiently treat a greater number of patients. Also, increased private financial support promised opportunities for extended hospital services and research.

Economically, however, the 1930s were dismal. Banks failed and bankruptcies were commonplace, causing unemployment to soar. With their jobs gone, many people for the first time in their lives faced poverty and turned to state and local welfare agencies for aid. City Hospital was one such agency, and providing adequate medical care for the growing numbers of indigent citizens put a great strain on its resources.

Despite these difficult times the hospital achieved many successes in the 1930s. The first iron lung in the state was installed at City Hospital, a gift of Eli Lilly and Company. (The iron lung was the only known means of defeating infantile paralysis when it threatened to paralyze the lung muscles.) The hospital's 1936 annual report listed the purchase of three new lightweight, panel-body ambulances. Seven surgery rooms were equipped with air conditioning after early reports of a summer heat wave prompted a $10,000 gift from an anonymous Indianapolis philanthropist. The previous summer had been intensely hot, and throughout the city there were many cases of heat prostration. A cancer clinic opened in 1938, offering free diagnosis and treatment of the disease. In 1942 the American College of Surgeons gave high marks to the hospital for this program.

Patients admitted to City Hospital fell into three categories. The first was the free patient who had no available resources for medical treatment. The second was designated a part-pay patient, someone able to pay a small fee. The full-pay patient had the ability to pay all medical or surgical costs or had insurance or other means that would cover such costs.

The problem of insufficient public funds and public concern for the hospital's mission always existed. Fortunately, the generous and timely financial contributions of individuals and organizations advanced the good work being done by the staff. Without these private contributors, City Hospital, dependent solely on tax support, would not have gained the recognition it justly deserved for its successes in many areas of medicine.

The 1940s was s significant decade for medicine. It was at that time that miracle drugs came into being. Penicillin, discovered in 1926 by Sir Arthur Fleming, was widely available for medical use by the mid-1940s. Streptomycin and sulfa drugs came along early in the same decade. After World War II heart surgery became more common, and new drugs for hypertension came on the market.

When the United States went to war in 1941, City Hospital felt the impact. The 1943 annual report noted the marked reduction in the size of the staff because of the war. Not only were there fewer doctors on the visiting staff, but many of the younger men had also entered military service. The hospital averted a serious crisis by accepting twice the number of interns in 1942.

In 1943 two-way radios were installed in City Hospital ambulances. The hospital was the first in the nation to use this type of radio to coordinate ambulance dispatch. Because of wartime restrictions, radios were installed in only three of five hospital ambulances, but in time all would have them. With the ability to send as well as receive messages, ambulance doctors could now alert the receiving ward as to the nature of injury or illness of the patient coming in. Another innovation came in 1947 with the introduction of musical therapy—the piping of music and carefully selected radio programs into the psychiatric ward.

The introduction of health insurance coverage at City Hospital came in September 1944 when a rep-

resentative of Blue Cross of Indiana met with the hospital board. Blue Cross had been established in Indiana earlier that year. Its focus at that time was extremely limited: to pay hospital bills in accordance with membership agreements and participating hospital contracts. Myers, doubtful that the board should enter into a contract with Blue Cross, did suggest that both parties simply agree in writing to accept payment from Blue Cross for hospital services to Blue Cross members. It was an idea whose time had come.

GENERAL HOSPITAL, 1947–1975

In 1947 City Hospital was renamed Indianapolis General Hospital, but its role as a public hospital was not altered. It became Marion County General Hospital in 1951 when its services were extended to residents of the county. In the twenty-eight years the hospital was known as General Hospital, much progress was made, both in services provided for patient care and in medical research and education.

On 14 June 1950 Dr. Palmer Eicher, an orthopedic surgeon, performed the first hip replacement. A graduate of the Indiana University School of Medicine, Eicher had served his internship at City Hospital. His interest in orthopedic surgery began during his service with the Army Medical Corps in World War II. Later, as a member of the medical school's department of orthopedic surgery, he continued his study of hip replacements, pioneering the development of the stemmed femoral head implant, a concept that was the forerunner of present-day hip replacements.

Established by a 1951 act of the Indiana General Assembly, the Marion County Health and Hospital Corporation assumed responsibility for the medical

Easter Bunny visiting the pediatric ward.

care of the indigent, previously a function of the township trustee. In effect, it joined three entities: a municipal hospital, a public health division for the city and county, and an executive division coordinating the activities of those two.

Also in 1951 General Hospital gained recognition as one of thirty training centers in the nation and the only one in Indiana accredited to provide a three-year course for specialized training in skin diseases. The Robert Moore Heart Clinic, established in 1952, was an outgrowth of one of the hospital's earliest efforts in outpatient treatment of heart

patients. Later this cardiac clinic became a permanent part of the hospital's outpatient care and was incorporated into the curriculum at the Indiana University School of Medicine.

General Hospital was designated by the Indiana State Board of Health as a major trauma center for Indiana in 1969, implementing a comprehensive program that involved a wide range of activities relating to the cause and effects of trauma. Total care of the patient was the program's primary emphasis, and it required the coordination of many of the hospital's facilities. Foremost, of course, was the ambulance service. Also involved in this combined-care effort were the services of the emergency room, the surgical department, the intensive care unit, and rehabilitation. The nation's largest community mental health center opened at the hospital in February 1969, financed by federal and local funds. Part of a nationwide program for such centers, it was the first comprehensive mental health clinic in Indiana.

From the late 1940s until the mid-1970s, the hospital continued to provide good medical care and focused on three important issues: the institution's growth and development, its health-care mission and the public's perception of that, and its funding and management. Similar to its predecessor City Hospital, General was plagued with municipal politics and limited revenues and was greatly dependent on public funds.

In the late 1960s General Hospital and the Indiana University School of Medicine signed a letter of agreement that authorized the university to operate all of the intern and residency education programs at the hospital. This early agreement, which recognized the importance of internships and residencies in a combined program, was the first of several important alliances between the two institutions. As a public hospital caring for hundreds of patients a day, General Hospital offered its post-graduate students many opportunities other hospitals could not. Medical students at General saw not only the sick and injured patients admitted to the hospital but also the many who came to outpatient clinics.

Already accredited by the Indiana State Board of Nurses Registration and Nursing Education, the General Hospital School of Nursing in 1962 received national recognition by the National League for Nursing. General Hospital's nursing program had much to offer prospective nurses, and by 1962 it had graduated more than fifteen hundred students. The hospital's use of emergency medical technicians began early in the 1970s. EMTs were trained in basic life support, including the recognition and management of trauma, cardiopulmonary resuscitation, shock management, control of bleeding, and similar emergency care.

In 1975 General Hospital, under terms of a new agreement between the Health and Hospital Corporation Trustees and the Indiana University board of trustees, began an even closer affiliation with the Indiana University School of Medicine. The new contract called for the school of medicine to furnish management and professional services, including patient care, teaching, and research activities. The university was charged with expanding research facilities at General Hospital within the limits of General's physical and financial boundaries. It was also to negotiate all future arrangements, agreements, or contracts with parties providing services to the hospital. Under terms of the contract, the board of trustees of Marion County Health and Hospital Corporation retained the ultimate responsibility for institutions, policies, and programs. This arrangement benefited the medical school as well as the hospital. The school needed large numbers of patients, and General could provide those patients. One purpose of the new management contract was to make outstanding medical care available to all in need of it and, as a consequence, to attract more private patients to the hospital.

Perhaps it was inevitable with this intended re-imaging of the hospital that the hospital's name also be changed. The board of trustees of the Health and Hospital Corporation chose to pay tribute to Dr. William Niles Wishard, in whose honor the hospital was renamed on 19 September 1975. The board considered it an opportunity to give the hospital a name that had historical relevancy and also recognized the importance of the Wishard years.

In 1978 the Joint Commission on Accreditation of Hospitals for the first time awarded Wishard Hospital an A+ rating. Wishard was one of fewer than two hundred hospitals given this honor. The School of Nursing graduated its last class in 1980, one hundred years after its founding by the Flower Mission, and was the last of the hospital nursing schools in the city.

In 1985 the contract with the school of medicine was rewritten, and while the Health and Hospital Corporation controlled the hospital, the medical school became its agent. As time went on, these two entities investigated new solutions to the never-ending problem of balancing costs and income. In the 1990s Wishard adopted a radical concept in health-care delivery, centering less on the hospital's role and more on the patient's need. From this evolved the more broadly named Wishard Health Services.

WISHARD MEMORIAL HOSPITAL TODAY

In the early twenty-first century, Wishard Memorial Hospital (renamed in 1975 and today called Wishard Health Services) finds itself in a strong position. The physical plant is in better condition than it has ever been. New and renovated buildings and driveways have improved the appearance of the hospital grounds.

While the majority of its patients are tax supported, the hospital also attracts commercially insured patients. Wishard has been identified as a top-100 hospital for three consecutive years in a national ranking. Many public hospitals across the country have been phased out or are in danger of being closed, but Wishard Hospital continues. Its long and close connection with the Indiana University School of Medicine, and the strength of its leadership, have placed this hospital well ahead of comparable institutions in the United States. While Wishard benefits by being a teaching hospital, it also serves as a very valuable asset to the medical school. Both the university and the hospital gain from this important alliance.

Wishard provides a 260-bed hospital for inpatients and treats more than 900,000 outpatients every year. While the adult burn unit and the trauma center are perhaps the two most highly recognized services of the hospital, as many as 1,500 people may come to its clinics in a single day. Six community health centers offer neighborhood medical care. The Midtown Community Mental Health program provides mental health and counseling services in outreach centers and assisted living homes. Eighteen ambulances are ready on call. The bulk of Wishard patients, perhaps 60 percent, are unexpected, and a highly skilled emergency room staff is waiting, twenty-four hours a day, seven days a week, trained to deal with any crisis situation.

In offering a continuum of health care, Wishard Health Services now emphasizes many reasons for patients to choose Wishard, whether it be the emergency service, the primary care outpatient clinic, inpatient hospital care, long-term care, or any of the many other special Wishard programs. It proudly declares itself to be a health-care provider for patients of all ages and all periods of a person's life.

In all of its history, economics have governed Wishard Hospital's activity. But the hospital has always survived. Funding will continue to be challenging and all important. As federal and state monies become less available, there is greater pressure on city funds. Reduced Medicare and Medicaid funding presents a serious problem.

The hospital has continued to benefit from efficient, devoted management. Dr. John F. Williams, Jr., brought many changes during his decade as the hospital's director. His vision and enthusiasm helped reshape policies and attitudes at Wishard. Under his leadership, Wishard Health Services moved in new directions.

In September 1998 Williams retired. His successor was Dr. Randall L. Braddom, who served until 2000. The current director, Dr. Robert B. Jones, is a longtime Indiana University School of Medicine physician and has served as Associate Dean for Clinical Affairs and chief of the Division of Infectious Disease of the Department of Medicine. Prior to being appointed director of Wishard, Jones was executive vice president of Clarian Health Partners, Inc.

The public impression of Wishard is changing. Too often it has been thought of as a poor person's hospital, a place where no one but indigent people would go. Poor people were equated with poor health care.

More people now realize that Wishard's level of care is sophisticated. They recognize that medical care at Wishard is equal to the other hospitals whose patient population is considered financially more stable.

Wishard is committed to the efficient delivery of high quality health care and the promotion of wellness and health-care education. Wishard's commitment is to provide compassionate care for all of the sick and injured who come there, with no distinctions made because of ethnic or religious background, national origin, disability, or financial or social status. Throughout its history this has been the hospital's obligation, whether it was called City Hospital, General, or Wishard.

Dr. William Niles Wishard's vision led to an expanded City Hospital. Fully aware of the hospital's role and potential in Indianapolis, he challenged local government, medical colleagues, and the community at large with the importance of the hospital. Later superintendents continued to work for the hospital's growth, despite never-ending battles for sufficient funds to keep the hospital functioning. Challenges facing Wishard Health Services today are monumental in comparison to those experienced by these men. Yet Wishard persists in its work and does it well. Similar to City Hospital and General Hospital in earlier times, Wishard continues its commitment to provide the best possible care to all who come there in need of it.

APPENDIX 1: Catalog of the City Hospital Murals

J. OTTIS ADAMS
Whitewater at Brookville
29" x 35"
Oil on canvas adhered to Masonite

WISHARD ART COLLECTION
CONSERVATION BY SNODGRASS STUDIOS

J. OTTIS ADAMS
Whitewater at Brookville
29" x 35"
Oil on canvas adhered to Masonite

WISHARD ART COLLECTION
CONSERVATION BY SNODGRASS STUDIOS

WAYMAN ADAMS
Mary Vissa
23" x 19"
Oil on canvas

WISHARD ART COLLECTION
CONSERVATION BY IMA CONSERVATION
LAB

WAYMAN ADAMS
Tener Reko
23" x 19"
Oil on canvas adhered
to Masonite

WISHARD ART COLLECTION
CONSERVATION BY SNODGRASS STUDIOS

WAYMAN ADAMS
Richard William Etter
23" x 19"
Oil on canvas

WISHARD ART COLLECTION
CONSERVATION BY IMA CONSERVATION
LAB

WAYMAN ADAMS
Portrait of Child
23" x 19" (before canvas was cut down)
Oil on canvas adhered
to Masonite

WISHARD ART COLLECTION
CONSERVATION BY SNODGRASS STUDIOS

WAYMAN ADAMS
Portrait of Child
23" x 19"
Oil on canvas adhered
to Masonite

WISHARD ART COLLECTION
RESTORED BY EFFIE CARTER

WAYMAN ADAMS
Portrait of Child
23" x 19"
Oil on canvas adhered
to Masonite

WISHARD ART COLLECTION
RESTORED BY EFFIE CARTER

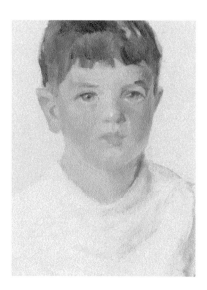

WAYMAN ADAMS
Portrait of Child
23" x 19" (before canvas was cut down)
Oil on canvas adhered
to Masonite

WISHARD ART COLLECTION
CONSERVATION BY SNODGRASS STUDIOS

WAYMAN ADAMS
Anna Marie Brodeur
23" x 19"
Oil on canvas adhered
to Masonite

WISHARD ART COLLECTION
CONSERVATION BY SNODGRASS STUDIOS

WAYMAN ADAMS
Portrait of Child
23" x 19" (before canvas was cut down)
Oil on canvas adhered
to Masonite

WISHARD ART COLLECTION
CONSERVATION BY SNODGRASS STUDIOS

WAYMAN ADAMS
Portrait of Child
23" x 19"
Oil on canvas adhered
to Masonite

MARTINUS ANDERSEN
Idealized Landscape
48" x 91"
Oil on canvas adhered to Masonite

MARTINUS ANDERSEN
Idealized Landscape
52" x 43"
Oil on canvas adhered to
Masonite

MARTINUS ANDERSEN
Idealized Landscape
53" x 106"
Oil on canvas adhered to Masonite

MARTINUS ANDERSEN
Idealized Landscape
43" x 91"
Oil on canvas adhered to Masonite

FRANCIS F. BROWN
Idealized Landscape
52" x 106"
Oil on canvas adhered to Masonite

JAY H. CONNAWAY
Landscape
38" x 60"
Oil on canvas adhered to Masonite

WISHARD ART COLLECTION
CONSERVATION BY SNODGRASS STUDIOS

JAY H. CONNAWAY
Landscape
38" x 59"
Oil on canvas adhered to Masonite

WISHARD ART COLLECTION
CONSERVATION BY SNODGRASS STUDIOS

WILLIAM FORSYTH
Two Children
35" x 34"
Oil on canvas adhered to Masonite

WISHARD ART COLLECTION
CONSERVATION BY SNODGRASS STUDIOS

CARL C. GRAF
The Three Muses
52" x 59"
Oil on canvas adhered to Masonite

WISHARD ART COLLECTION
CONSERVATION BY SNODGRASS STUDIOS

CARL C. GRAF
Landscape
53" x 43"
Oil on canvas adhered to Masonite

WILLIAM EDOUARD SCOTT
Simeon and the Babe Jesus
98" x 44"
Oil on canvas adhered to Masonite

WILLIAM EDOUARD SCOTT
Pilgrim Dwelling
68" x 110"
Oil on canvas adhered to Masonite

WILLIAM EDOUARD SCOTT
Pilgrim Dwelling
69" x 66"
Oil on canvas adhered to Masonite

WISHARD ART COLLECTION
CONSERVATION BY SNODGRASS STUDIOS

WILLIAM EDOUARD SCOTT
Two Indians
72" x 68"
Oil on canvas adhered to Masonite

WISHARD ART COLLECTION
CONSERVATION BY SNODGRASS STUDIOS

T. C. STEELE
Autumnal Landscape
72" x 35"
Oil on canvas adhered to Masonite

T. C. STEELE
Autumnal Landscape
72" x 35"
Oil on canvas adhered to Masonite

T. C. STEELE
Autumn Landscape with Path
72" x 35"
Oil on canvas adhered to Masonite

WISHARD ART COLLECTION • CONSERVATION BY SNODGRASS STUDIOS

T. C. STEELE
Four Seasons, Spring
60" x 111"
Oil on canvas adhered to Masonite

T. C. STEELE
Spring Trees
72" x 35"
Oil on canvas adhered to
Masonite

T. C. STEELE
Four Seasons, Summer
60" x 111"
Oil on canvas adhered to Masonite

T. C. STEELE
Four Seasons, Autumn
60" x 111"
Oil on canvas adhered to Masonite

WISHARD ART COLLECTION
CONSERVATION BY SNODGRASS STUDIOS

CLIFTON WHEELER
Idealized Landscape
52" x 43"
Oil on canvas adhered to Masonite

WISHARD ART COLLECTION
CONSERVATION BY SNODGRASS STUDIOS

T. C. STEELE
Four Seasons, Winter
60" x 111"
Oil on canvas adhered to Masonite

INDIANA STATE MUSEUM AND HISTORIC SITES

CLIFTON WHEELER
Idealized Landscape
43" x 52"
Oil on canvas adhered to Masonite

WISHARD ART COLLECTION
CONSERVATION BY SNODGRASS STUDIOS

CLIFTON WHEELER
Landscape with Lombardy Poplars
51" x 45"
Oil on canvas adhered to Masonite

WISHARD ART COLLECTION
CONSERVATION BY SNODGRASS STUDIOS

CLIFTON WHEELER
Women and Children
39" x 70"
Oil on canvas adhered to Masonite

WISHARD ART COLLECTION
CONSERVATION BY SNODGRASS STUDIOS

CLIFTON WHEELER
Nursery Rhymes
5 ¾" x 11 ½" (each panel)
Watercolor, mixed media on paper

T. C. STEELE
October
24" x 20"
Oil on canvas

APPENDIX 2: Burdsal Units by Floor

ORIG. FLOOR / LOCATION	PATIENT CARE FOCUS	ARTIST	MURAL NAME / SUBJECT	CURRENT DISPOSITION
entry to B / basement level		Helene Hibben	Burdsal dedication plaque	BA 2, Wishard Memorial Hospital
B basement	mental and nervous			not part of 1914 mural project
B-1 / hall, lobby, side rooms	women's surgical	Martinus Andersen	idealized landscapes	4 paintings, Wishard collection
B-1 / ward		T. C. Steele	Four Seasons / landscapes	7 paintings, Wishard collection; 1 painting, Indiana State Museum collection
B-1 / sunroom		J. Ottis Adams	landcapes	2 paintings, Wishard collection
B-2 / side room, ward	women's medical	Dorothy Morlan	idealized landscapes	1 photograph from early assessment, painting location unknown
B-2 / sunroom		Dorothy Morlan	idealized landscapes	
B-3 / lobby	women's medical, surgical, and obstetrics, African-American (later used as cancer ward)	Francis F. Brown	landscapes	1 painting, Wishard collection
B-3 / hall		Carl C. Graf	landscapes	1 painting, Wishard collection
B-3 / ward		Carl C. Graf	classical figures	1 figurative painting in the Wishard collection (*The Three Muses*); 2 photographs of paintings from earlier assessment, location unknown
B-3 / sunroom		Carl C. Graf	landscapes	
B-3 / private room		Emma B. King		presumed destroyed
B-3 side room		Simon Baus		presumed destroyed
B-4 / lobby	women's "miscellaneous" (later used as women's psychiatric ward)	William Edouard Scott	bibical scenes	presumed destroyed
B-4 / ward		William Edouard Scott	life of Jesus	1 painting, Wishard collection
C basement	men's medical and surgical, African-American			not part of 1914 mural project
C-1 / lobby	men's surgical	William Edouard Scott	Morning and Evening (classical figures)	presumed destroyed
C-1 / side room		William Edouard Scott	pilgrim scenes	3 paintings, Wishard Art Collection
C-1 / hall				no record of murals by 1948
C-1 / sunroom		William Edouard Scott	The Nations of the Earth Coming to the Light	presumed destroyed
C-1 / ward		William Edouard Scott	Four Seasons	presumed destroyed
C-2 / lobby	men's medical	Clifton Wheeler	idealized landscapes	1 painting, Wishard collection
C-2 / side room		Walter Hixon Isnogle	Classic figures	presumed destroyed
C-2 / hall and ward		Clifton Wheeler	landscapes	3 paintings, Wishard collection
C-2 / sunroom		Clifton Wheeler	farm scenes	presumed destroyed
C-3 / hall	pediatric	Carl C. Graf	Cinderella series	presumed destroyed
C-3 / hall		Carl C. Graf	Elfin Grove	presumed destroyed
C-3 / lobby		Walter Hixon Isnogle	Music, Literature, and Art	presumed destroyed
C-3 / dining room		Otto Stark	Parade of Toys	presumed destroyed
C-3 / ward		Wayman Adams	portraits of children	9 paintings, Wishard collection; 1 painting, Indianapolis Museum of Art
C-3 / sunroom		Clifton Wheeler	Fairy Tales: *Jack and the Beanstalk*; *The Pied Piper of Hamlin*; *The Goose Girl*; *Little Red Riding Hood*	presumed destroyed
C-4 / all areas	pediatrics and premature infants	William Forsyth	children in natural settings	1 painting, Wishard collection, remainder on walls in BA-5, Wishard Hospital

ORIG. FLOOR / LOCATION	PATIENT CARE FOCUS	ARTIST	MURAL NAME / SUBJECT	CURRENT DISPOSITION
occupational therapy		Clifton Wheeler and Otto Stark	Fairy Tales: *Rock-a-Bye Baby*; *Ding, Dong Bell*; *Simple Simon*; *Tom, Tom the Piper's Son*; *Mary, Mary Quite Contrary*; *Pussy Cat, Pussy Cat, Where Have You Been?*; *Hark, Hark! The Dogs Do Bark*; *Jack Be Nimble, Jack Be Quick*; *Little Bo Beep* [sic]; and *Little Boy Blue*	unknown, some may be in IPS schools
found during remodeling / unknown		Jay H. Connaway	landscapes	2 paintings, Wishard collection

APPENDIX 3: The Children in Wayman Adams's Portraits

1. Antonivich, Olivia (Serbian)—age 4; daughter of Mr. and Mrs. Nicholas Antonivich
2. Baby Abbot (Caucasian)—son of Dr. and Mrs. Frank E. Abbot; Mrs. Abbot was one of the founders and the first president of the St. Margaret's Hospital Guild
3. Bennett, Puryear (African America)—grandson of John A. Puryear
4. Brodeur, Anna Marie (French)—age 6; daughter of Mr. and Mrs. Theodore Paul Brodeur*
5. Day, Robert (Caucasian)—son of Mr. and Mrs. Frank Day; Mrs. Day was the niece of Dr. T. B. Eastman, a member of the City Board of Health
6. Dorsey, Harry Joseph (Irish)—age 6; son of Mr. and Mrs. James Dorsey
7. Etter, Richard William (German)*
8. Fletcher, Stoughton Jr. (Caucasian)—son of Mr. and Mrs. Stoughton Fletcher; Stoughton Fletcher was a prominent banker
9. Gatto, Rosario (Italian)—son of Mr. and Mrs. Rosario Gatto
10. Jackson, Mildred (Caucasian)—daughter of Dr. and Mrs. J. B. Jackson, member of the City Board of Health
11. Linkhow, Rosa (Jewish)—age 13 months; daughter of Mr. and Mrs. Louis Linkhow
12. Lung, Newton (Chinese)—son of E. Lung, laundryman
13. Lupear, George (Romanian)—son of Mr. and Mrs. George Lupear
14. Maddalena, Mamie (Italian)—age 6; daughter of Concettina Maddalena
15. Marshall, Marian (Caucasian)—daughter of Dr. and Mrs. Augustus L. Marshall, close friend of Dr. T. Victor Keene
16. Mastropolo, Agnes (Italian)—daughter of Mr. and Mrs. Alellia Mastropolo
17. Mendelsohn, Raphael (Russian Jew)—age 6; daughter of Mr. and Mrs. Lazareth Mendelsohn
18. Morgan, Jackson (Caucasian)—son of Dr. and Mrs. Herman G. Morgan, city health officer
19. Navrofrides, Elsie (Greek)—daughter of Mr. and Mrs. Evangel Navrofrides
20. Paton, Charles Lewis Duddington (Scottish)—son of Mr. and Mrs. George C. Paton
21. Reko, Tener (Hungarian)—age 5; daughter of Mr. and Mrs. C. X. Pono Reko
22. Reinne, Paul (Danish German)—son of Mr. and Mrs. Herman Reinne
23. Russ, Lorentia Mary (Hungarian)—age 6; daughter of Mr. and Mrs. Peter Russ
24. Vissa, Mary (Croatian)—age 6; daughter of Mr. and Mrs. John Vissa*
25. Ward, Joseph Henry (African American)—son of Dr. and Mrs. Joseph Ward

*Painting is part of the current Wishard collection.

This list compiled from:
   Thurman B. Rice, "History of the Medical Campus Chapter XXII: The Mural Paintings at General Hospital," *Monthly Bulletin Indiana State Board of Health* 51 (Oct. 1948): 235–39.
Indianapolis Star, 30 Aug. 1914.

NOTES

NOTES FOR CATLIN-LEGUTKO ESSAY

1. The hospital was known as City Hospital from 1859 to 1947 when it was changed to Indianapolis General Hospital. In 1951 it was renamed Marion County General Hospital, and in 1975 it was changed to Wishard Memorial Hospital. With the expansion of services into community-based clinics, the organization became known as Wishard Health Services.

2. William Forsyth, *Art in Indiana* (Indianapolis: H. Lieber, 1916), 23.

3. Mary Q. Burnet, *Art and Artists of Indiana* (New York: Century Co., 1921), 180.

4. A yellow, crystalline, volatile substance, having an offensive odor and sweetish taste, and analogous to chloroform. It is used in medicine as a healing and antiseptic dressing for wounds and sores.

5. Hester Anne Hale, *Caring for the Community: The History of Wishard Hospital* (Indianapolis: Wishard Memorial Foundation, 1999).

6. Burnet, *Art and Artists of Indiana*, 180–81.

7. Charles A. Bonsett, "Medical Museum Notes," *Indiana Medicine: The Journal of the Indiana State Medical Association* 81 (Sept. 1988): 748.

8. Thurman B. Rice, "History of the Medical Campus Chapter XXII: The Mural Paintings at General Hospital," *Monthly Bulletin Indiana State Board of Health* 51 (Oct. 1948): 235.

9. *Architectural and Historic Study Area* (Indianapolis: Historic Landmarks Foundation of Indiana, 1990).

10. These buildings are also known as the BU and BA buildings.

11. *Indianapolis News*, 28 Nov. 1914.

12. Ibid., 25 Nov. 1914.

13. *Indianapolis Star*, 7 Jan. 1940.

14. Bonsett, Hale, and Rice report that the gift was two hundred dollars, while an *Indianapolis Star* article of 7 January 1940 and Burnet's 1921 book state that the amount was one thousand dollars. Whatever the sum, it was small considering the scale of the completed project.

15. *Indianapolis Star*, 7 Jan. 1940.

16. In a 1948 article Rice reported that a committee was appointed consisting of T. C. Steele, J. Ottis Adams, William Forsyth, and Otto Stark, and these artists offered the mural project as a counterproposal to the Guild's idea of purchasing a single painting. This is the only article to discuss such a committee of artists. Forsyth recounts a meeting between Clifton Wheeler, Carl C. Graf, and Dr. T. Victor Keene. The 7 January 1940 *Indianapolis Star* reported a meeting between Keene, Wheeler, and Adams. It is the latter story that is most likely because Keene is heavily quoted in the *Star*'s article.

17. *Indianapolis Star*, 7 Jan. 1940.

18. Rice, "History of the Medical Campus," 236.

19. Fred D. Cavinder, "The Murals of Wishard," *Indianapolis Star Magazine*, 29 Apr. 1984, p. 12.

20. This list of artists added to the four committee members equals sixteen artists. Most accounts refer to fifteen participating artists, but the names on the list often change. Most frequently, Simon Baus is not listed.

21. Rice, "History of the Medical Campus," 236; *Indianapolis Star*, 7 Jan. 1940; Betty Lane, "Clifton Wheeler: Rekindled Appreciation," *Indianapolis Star Magazine*, 2 Nov. 1980, p. 46.

22. *Indianapolis News*, 28 Nov. 1914.

23. Rice, "History of the Medical Campus," 238.

24. *Indianapolis Star*, 7 Jan. 1940.

25. Ibid.

26. *Indianapolis News*, 28 Nov. 1914.

27. Forsyth, *Art in Indiana*, 23.

28. *Indianapolis News*, 28 Nov. 1914.

29. Rice, "History of the Medical Campus," 235.

30. The Burdsal wards were numbered BB, B-1, B-2, B-3, B-4, and the same series for the C wards. Today, the floors are numbered BU 1–5 and BA 1–5.

31. Judith Vale Newton, *The Hoosier Group: Five American Painters* (Indianapolis: Eckert Publications, 1985). Discussions regarding the Hoosier Group artists J. Ottis Adams, William Forsyth, Otto Stark, and T. C. Steele were derived primarily from this text.

32. Rice, "History of the Medical Campus," 238.

33. Overpainting is the outdated conservation technique of adding a layer(s) of paint over an artist's original painting. This was done to restore its original aesthetic, but it tends to alter a painting's appearance. Putty is used to build up the surface of a painting if there have been rips and tears. In the case of the City Hospital murals overpainting and putty were used heavily because the murals sustained serious damage when they were removed from the walls. Effective conservators focus on reversible techniques and processes such as wax fills and subtle inpainting.

34. Newton, *Hoosier Group*.

35. The panic was due to an economic reversal that began in Europe and reached the United States in fall 1873. The New York Stock Exchange was closed for ten days, banks failed, foreclosures and unemployment rose, and many Americans were financially ruined. The economy did not recover until 1878.

36. Selma N. Steele, Theodore L. Steele, and Wilbur D. Peat, *The House of the Singing Winds: The Life and Work of T. C. Steele* (Indianapolis: Indiana Historical Society, 1966), 147.

37. Alfred M. Brooks, "The Art and Work of Theodore C. Steele," *American Art Magazine* 8, no. 10 (Aug. 1917): 405.

38. William H. Walsh, *The Hospitals of Indianapolis: A Survey* (Indianapolis: Indianapolis Foundation, 1930), 31.

39. Newton, *Hoosier Group*.

40. *Indianapolis Star*, 7 Jan. 1940.

41. Newton, *Hoosier Group*.

42. *Indianapolis News*, 28 Nov. 1914.

43. *Indianapolis Star*, 1937, clipping, Artists' Files, Indianapolis Museum of Art (hereafter cited as IMA files).

44. *Indianapolis News*, 6 Feb. 1936.

45. *Indianapolis Star*, 1937, clipping, IMA files.

46. Wilbur D. Peat, *Wayman Adams: Memorial Exhibition of Paintings* (Indianapolis: John Herron Art Institute, 1959).

47. Burnet, *Art and Artists of Indiana*, 244–45.

48. *Indianapolis Star*, 30 Aug. 1914.

49. Rice, "History of the Medical Campus," 239.

50. Anne F. Clapp and Paul Spheeris, *Murals at Indianapolis General Hospital* (Oberlin, Ohio: Intermuseum Laboratory, 1967).

51. Burnet, *Art and Artists of Indiana*, 246.

52. Peat, *Wayman Adams*.

53. William E. Taylor, "Echoes of the Past: Artists' Biographies," in *A Shared Heritage: Art by Four African Americans*, edited by William E. Taylor and Harriet G. Warkel (Indianapolis: Indianapolis Museum of Art in cooperation with Indiana University Press, 1996), 160–66.

54. Ibid., 160.

55. William E. Taylor, "William Edouard Scott: Indianapolis Painter," *Black History News & Notes* 33 (Aug. 1988): 5.

56. Harriet G. Warkel, "A Shared Heritage: The Art of William Edouard Scott, John W. Hardrick, and Hale A. Woodruff," *Traces of Indiana and Midwestern History* 8, no. 1 (winter 1996): 42.

57. *Indianapolis Star*, 31 Oct. 1915.

58. Tanner was the first artist to depict the black experience but later turned to religious themes.

59. *Indianapolis Star*, 31 Oct. 1915.

60. Edmund Barry Gaither, "The Mural Tradition," in Taylor and Warkel, eds., *Shared Heritage*, 129.

61. Ibid.

62. *Indianapolis Star*, 7 Jan. 1940.

63. Gaither, "Mural Tradition," 129.

64. Rice, "History of the Medical Campus," 236.

65. This is the same painting as *Christ with Simeon*. Wishard's records refer to it as *Simeon and the Babe Jesus*.

66. *Indianapolis Star*, 31 Oct. 1915, 7 Jan. 1940.

67. Rice, "History of the Medical Campus," 237.

68. *Indianapolis Star*, 7 Jan. 1940; Cavinder, "Murals of Wishard," 12.

69. Rice, "History of the Medical Campus," 237.

70. *Indianapolis News*, 28 Nov. 1914.

71. *Indianapolis Star*, 31 Oct. 1915.

72. Rice, "History of the Medical Campus," 236.

73. Margaret T. G. Burroughs, "The Four Artists," in Taylor and Warkel, eds., *Shared Heritage*, 13.

74. Lyn Letsinger-Miller, *The Artists of Brown County* (Bloomington and Indianapolis: Indiana University Press, 1994), 124.

75. *Indianapolis News*, 17 Jan. 1925.

76. Letsinger-Miller, *Artists of Brown County*, 124.

77. *Indianapolis Star*, 7 Jan. 1940.

78. Rice, "History of the Medical Campus," 236, 237.

79. Walsh, *Hospitals of Indianapolis*, 31.

80. *Indianapolis Star*, 7 Jan. 1940.

81. Rice, "History of the Medical Campus," 236.

82. *Indianapolis News*, 28 Nov. 1914.

83. *Indianapolis Star*, 7 Jan. 1940.

84. *Indianapolis News*, 28 Nov. 1914.

85. Letsinger-Miller, *Artists of Brown County*, 127–31.

86. Walsh, *Hospitals of Indianapolis*, 31; Rice, "History of the Medical Campus," 237.

87. Lane, "Clifton Wheeler," 45.

88. Paul R. Martin, "Pretty European Romance Develops while Hoosier Is Studying in Italy, France and Germany and Marries Daughter of American Magazine Editor," unidentified clipping, IMA files.

89. Harriet G. Warkel, "The Herron School of Art Centennial," *American Art Review* 14, no. 6 (Nov.–Dec. 2002): 90.

90. Martin, "Pretty European Romance Develops while Hoosier Is Studying in Italy, France and Germany."

91. Warkel, "Herron School of Art Centennial," 90.

92. Patte Owings, "Clifton Wheeler," in *Exhibition of the Irvington Group of Artists, 1928–1937* (Indianapolis: Irvington Historical Society and Indianapolis–Marion County Public Library, 1984), 33.

93. Rice, "History of the Medical Campus," 237.

94. *Indianapolis News*, 28 Nov. 1914.

95. Rice, "History of the Medical Campus," 237.

96. *Indianapolis Star*, 1937, clipping, IMA files.

97. Rice, "History of the Medical Campus," 237.

98. *Indianapolis News*, 19 Aug. 1916.

99. Lane, "Clifton Wheeler," 44–46.

100. Walsh, *Hospitals of Indianapolis*; Rice, "History of the Medical Campus," 236.

101. *Indianapolis News*, 28 Nov. 1914.

102. Burnet, *Art and Artists of Indiana*, 251.

103. *Indianapolis News*, 28 Nov. 1914.

104. *Indianapolis Star*, Nov. 1915, clipping, IMA files.

105. Lois Leamon, "Simon Baus," in *Exhibition of the Irvington Group of Artists*, 15.

106. Burnet, *Art and Artists of Indiana*, 248.

107. *Indianapolis News*, 28 Nov. 1914.

108. *Ball State (Muncie) Daily News*, 15 Apr. 1971.

109. Walsh, *Hospitals of Indianapolis*; Rice, "History of the Medical Campus," 236.

110. James Ong, *The Hoosier Art Collection of the Kokomo–Howard County Public Library* (Kokomo: Kokomo–Howard County Public Library, 1989), 11.

111. *National Cyclopedia of American Biography*, 63 vols. (New York: J. T. White, 1930–78), 55:339–40.

112. Charles G. Wilson, "The Maine Years of Jay Connaway, Sea Painter," *Down East Magazine* (June 1965).

113. Ibid.

114. *Indianapolis News*, 13 July 1967.

115. Rice, "History of the Medical Campus," 236.

116. Sheri A. Patterson, "Helene Hibben," in *Exhibition of the Irvington Group of Artists*, 23.

117. *Indianapolis News*, 28 Nov. 1914.

118. *Indianapolis Star*, 29 May 1916.

119. Ibid., 7 Jan. 1940.

120. *Indianapolis News*, 28 Nov. 1914.

121. Burnet, *Art and Artists of Indiana*, 249.

122. *Indianapolis Star*, 18 July 1933.

123. *Indianapolis News*, 28 Nov. 1914.

124. Virginia Lucas Finney, "Dorothy Morlan: Dreamer of Landscapes," unidentified clipping, 26 Apr. 1976, IMA files.

125. Rice, "History of the Medical Campus," 236.

126. *Indianapolis News*, 28 Nov. 1914.

127. Rice, "History of the Medical Campus," 236–37.
128. *Indianapolis News,* 28 Nov. 1914.
129. *Indianapolis Star,* 31 Oct. 1915.
130. Forsyth, *Art in Indiana,* 23.
131. *Indianapolis Star,* 7 Jan. 1940.
132. Brooks, "Art and Work of Theodore Steele," 405.
133. Clapp and Spheeris, *Murals at Indianapolis General Hospital.*
134. *Indianapolis News,* 28 Nov. 1914.
135. Clapp and Spheeris, *Murals at Indianapolis General Hospital.*
136. Ibid.
137. "The Murals of City Hospital," *Wishard Today* 1, no.1 (Mar.–Apr. 1980): 3; *Indianapolis News,* 13 July 1967.

138. Linda Witkowski, Reports of the Wishard Art Collection, 2003, Indianapolis Museum of Art and Wishard Health Services.
139. Anu Kasarabada, "Art Depreciation," *Indianapolis Monthly* (Apr. 2003): 32.
140. Martin Radecki, conservation discussions, May 2003, Indianapolis Museum of Art.
141. *Progress Report* (Indianapolis: Marion County General Art Evaluation and Study Committee, 1975).
142. Richard Lowery to Carl H. Armstrong, 21 June 1976, archives, Wishard Nursing Museum, Indianapolis, Ind.
143. Gloria Gresham to Chester Smith, 3 Feb. 1977, ibid.

NOTES FOR NAGLER ESSAY
1. Mary Q. Burnet, *Art and Artists of Indiana* (New York: Century Co., 1921), 182.
2. William Forsyth, *Art in Indiana* (Indianapolis: H. Lieber, 1916), 23.
3. William H. Gerdts, *American Impressionism* (New York and London: Abbeville Press, 1984), 147.
4. Ibid.
5. Martin Krause, *The Passage: Return of Indiana Painters from Germany, 1880–1905* (Indianapolis: Indianapolis Museum of Art, 1990), 126.
6. Ibid.
7. Gerdts, *American Impressionism,* 147.
8. Krause, *Passage,* 123.
9. Judith Vale Newton, *The Hoosier Group: Five American Painters* (Indianapolis: Eckert Publications, 1985), 43; Krause, *Passage,* 123.
10. Krause, *Passage,* 124.
11. Gerdts, *American Impressionism,* 142.
12. Ibid.
13. Ibid.
14. Forsyth, *Art in Indiana,* 23.
15. Ibid.
16. Robert M. Taylor, Jr., "'Some Special Object:' The Arts and Crafts Society of Indianapolis," *Traces of Indiana and Midwestern History* 6, no. 1 (winter 1994): 22–27.
17. Gerdts, *American Impressionism,* 337.
18. Forsyth, *Art in Indiana,* 23.
19. Ibid.
20. Ibid.

BIBLIOGRAPHY

Books

Architectural and Historic Study Area. Indianapolis: Historic Landmarks Foundation of Indiana, 1990.

Art Collection by Indiana Artists. Indianapolis: IAC Arts Foundation, 1994.

Bailey, Dorothy Birney, comp. and ed. *Brown County Remembers.* Nashville, Ind.: Revere Press, 1986.

Battista, Sharon D. *Condition and Assessment Report of Wishard Collection.* Indianapolis, 1992.

Brown County Art and Artists. Nashville, Ind.: Psi Iota Xi, 1971.

Burnet, Mary Q. *Art and Artists of Indiana.* New York: Century Co., 1921.

Bustin, Dillon. *If You Don't Outdie Me: The Legacy of Brown County.* Bloomington: Indiana University Press, 1982.

Clapp, Anne F., and Paul Spheeris. *Murals at Indianapolis General Hospital.* Oberlin, Ohio: Intermuseum Laboratory, 1967.

Drawings by the Hoosier Group. Muncie, Ind.: Ball State University, 1976.

Exhibition of Paintings by Francis Brown. Richmond, Ind.: Public Art Gallery, 1918.

Exhibition of the Irvington Group of Artists, 1928–1937. Indianapolis: Irvington Historical Society and Indianapolis–Marion County Public Library, 1984.

Five Hoosier Painters: Being a Discussion of the Holiday Exhibit of the Indianapolis Group in Chicago. Chicago: Central Art Association, 1894.

Forsyth, William. *Art in Indiana.* Indianapolis: H. Lieber, 1916.

Gerdts, William H. *Theodore Clement Steele: An American Master of Light.* New York: Chameleon Books, 1995.

Griner, Ned H. *J. Ottis Adams: A Sense of Place.* Muncie, Ind.: Minnetrista Cultural Foundation, 1985.

Hale, Hester Anne. *Caring for the Community: The History of Wishard Hospital.* Indianapolis: Wishard Memorial Foundation, 1999.

John Ottis and Winifred Brady Adams, Painters. Muncie, Ind.: Ball State University Art Gallery, 1976.

Krause, Martin F. *The Passage: Return of Indiana Painters from Germany, 1880–1905.* Indianapolis: Indianapolis Museum of Art, 1990.

———, and Mary Elizabeth Steele. *Realities and Impressions: Indiana Artists in Munich, 1880–1890.* Indianapolis: Indianapolis Museum of Art, 1985.

Lauter, Flora. *Indiana Artists (Active), 1940.* Spencer, Ind.: Samuel R. Guard and Co., 1941.

Letsinger-Miller, Lyn. *The Artists of Brown County.* Bloomington and Indianapolis: Indiana University Press, 1994.

Marine Paintings by Connaway. New York: Kennedy Galleries. Artists' Files, Indianapolis Museum of Art.

Milkovich, Michael. Introduction to *Jay Connaway: Fifty Years of His Works, 1919–1969.* Binghampton, N.Y.: University Art Gallery, 1969.

Mirages of Memory: Two Hundred Years of Indiana Art. Indianapolis: Indianapolis Museum of Art, 1977.

National Cyclopedia of Biography. Vol. 55. New York: J. T. White, 1974.

Nesbit, M. Joanne, ed., and Barbara Judd, comp. *Those Brown County Artists: The Ones Who Came, the Ones Who Stayed, the Ones Who Moved On, 1900–1950.* Nashville, Ind.: Nana's Books, 1993.

Newton, Judith Vale. *The Hoosier Group: Five American Painters.* Indianapolis: Eckert Publications, 1985.

———, and Carol Weiss. *A Grand Tradition: The Art and Artists of the Hoosier Salon, 1925–1990.* Indianapolis: Hoosier Salon Patrons Association, 1993.

Northway, Martin. *The Artists of Brown County and Where to Find Them.* Nashville, Ind.: Northway and Ranivaldt, 1979.

One Hundred Fifty Years of Indiana Art. Muncie, Ind.: Ball State University Art Gallery, 1966.

Ong, James. *The Hoosier Art Collection of the Kokomo–Howard County Public Library.* Kokomo, Ind.: Kokomo–Howard County Public Library, 1989.

Patton, Sharon F. *African-American Art.* New York: Oxford University Press, 1998.

Peat, Wilbur D. *Clifton Wheeler: Memorial Exhibition of Paintings.* Indianapolis: John Herron Art Museum, 1953.

———. *Pioneer Painters of Indiana.* Indianapolis: Art Association of Indianapolis, 1954.

———. *Wayman Adams: Memorial Exhibition of Paintings.* Indianapolis: John Herron Art Institute, 1959.

Perisho, Sally. *Woodruff, Hardrick, and Scott.* Indianapolis: Indianapolis Museum of Art, 1977.

Progress Report. Indianapolis: Marion County General Art Evaluation and Study Committee, 1975.

Steele, Selma N., Theodore L. Steele, and Wilbur D. Peat. *The House of the Singing Winds: The Life and Work of T. C. Steele.* Indianapolis: Indiana Historical Society, 1966.

T. C. Steele State Memorial. Indianapolis: Indiana Department of Natural Resources, 1976.

Taylor, William E., and Harriet G. Warkel, eds. *A Shared Heritage: Art by Four African Americans.* Indianapolis: Indianapolis Museum of Art in cooperation with Indiana University Press, 1996.

Walsh, William H. *The Hospitals of Indianapolis: A Survey.* Indianapolis: Indianapolis Foundation, 1930.

Periodicals, manuscripts, and reports

Bonsett, Charles A. "Medical Museum Notes." *Indiana Medicine: Journal of the Indiana State Medical Association* 81 (September 1988).

Brooks, Alfred M. "The Art and Work of Theodore C. Steele." *American Art Magazine* 8, no. 10 (August 1917).

Cavinder, Fred. "The Murals of Wishard." *Indianapolis Star Magazine,* 29 April 1984.

———. "Otto Stark: Salute to a Hoosier Artist." *Indianapolis Star Magazine,* 3 April 1977.

Driskell, David C. "Art by Blacks: Its Vital Role in U.S. Culture."

Smithsonian (October 1976).

Finney, Virgina Lucas. "Dorothy Morlan: Dreamer of Landscapes." Unidentified clipping, 26 April 1976. Artists' Files, Indianapolis Museum of Art.

Gresham, Gloria to Chester Smith, 3 February 1977. Archives, Wishard Nursing Museum, Indianapolis, Ind.

"Hospital Murals Still on Display." *Life in General* (September 1970).

"Indiana Artists Series: J. Ottis Adams." *New Era Magazine.* Artists' Files, Indianapolis Museum of Art.

"Jay Connaway." *Art Digest* (15 December 1937).

Kasarabada, Anu. "Art Depreciation." *Indianapolis Monthly* (April 2003).

Lane, Betty. "Clifton Wheeler: Rekindled Appreciation." *Indianapolis Star Magazine,* 2 November 1980.

"Local Museums Now Housing Hospital's Murals." *Life in General* (December 1970).

Lowery, Richard to Carl H. Armstrong, 21 June 1976. Archives, Wishard Nursing Museum, Indianapolis, Ind.

Martin, Paul R. "Pretty European Romance Develops while Hoosier Is Studying in Italy, France and Germany and Marries Daughter of American Magazine Editor." Unidentified undated clipping, Artists' Files, Indianapolis Museum of Art.

"Mr. Forsyth's Exhibit." *Illustrated Indiana Weekly,* 2 December 1899.

"The Murals of City Hospital." *Wishard Today* 1, no. 1 (March–April 1980).

Radecki, Martin. Interview with author, May 2003. Indianapolis Museum of Art.

Rice, Thurman B. "History of the Medical Campus Chapter XXII: The Mural Paintings at General Hospital." *Monthly Bulletin Indiana State Board of Health* 51 (October 1948).

Roberts, Peter J. "William Edouard Scott: Some Aspects of His Work." Photocopy. Report for Evelyn Mitchell's Afro-American Art Course at Emory University, 1988.

Taylor, William E. "William Edouard Scott: Indianapolis Painter." *Black History News & Notes* 33 (August 1988).

Warkel, Harriet G. "The Herron School of Art Centennial." *American Art Review* 14, no. 6 (November–December 2002).

———. "A Shared Heritage: The Art of William Edouard Scott, John W. Hardrick, and Hale A. Woodruff." *Traces of Indiana and Midwestern History* 8, no.1 (winter 1996).

Wilson, Charles G. "The Maine Years of Jay Connaway, Sea Painter." *Down East Magazine* (June 1995).

Witkowski, Linda. Reports of the Wishard Art Collection, 2003. Indianapolis Museum of Art and Wishard Health Services.

Newspapers (see individual citations in Notes)

Ball State (Muncie) Daily News, 1971.

Indianapolis News, 1914, 1916, 1925, 1937, 1967, 1978, 1990.

Indianapolis Star, 1910, 1912, 1913, 1914, 1915, 1919, 1920, 1926, 1933, 1937, 1940, 1941, 1943, 1947.

Indianapolis Times, 1920.

New York Post, 1934.

New York Sun, 1939.

New York Times, 1939.

New York Tribune, 1939.

Portland (Maine) Herald, 1934.